MW00681692

STECK-VAUGHN
Elements of Reading

Level C

Vocabulary

Isabel L. Beck, Ph.D., and Margaret G. McKeown, Ph.D.

Read-Aloud Anthology

HarcourtAchieve

Rigby · Steck-Vaughn

www.HarcourtAchieve.com

1.800.531.5015

Acknowledgments

Editorial Director Stephanie Muller

Lead Editor Terra Tarango

Editor Victoria Davis

Design Team Cynthia Ellis, Alexandra Corona, Joan Cunningham

Production Team Mychael Ferris-Pacheco, Paula Schumann, Alan Klemp

Editorial, Design, and Production Development The Quarasan Group, Inc.

Cover Illustration Lori Lohstoeter

Literature

Grateful acknowledgment is given to the following publishers and copyright owners for permissions granted to reprint selections from their publications. All possible care has been taken to trace ownership and secure permission for each selection included. In the case of any errors or omissions, the Publisher will be pleased to make suitable acknowledgments in future editions.

p. 1, WORDS ARE LIKE FACES by Edith Baer. Copyright © 1980 by Edith Baer. Reprinted by permission of the author.

p. 7, "Gloria Who Might Be My Best Friend" from THE STORIES JULIAN TELLS by Ann Cameron, illustrated by Ann Strugnell. Copyright © 1981 by Ann Cameron. Illustrations copyright © 1981 by Ann Strugnell. Used by permission of Alfred A. Knopf, an imprint of Random House Children's books, a division of Random House, Inc.

p. 15, HOW RABBIT LOST HIS TAIL by Ann Tompert, illustrated by Jacqueline Chwast. Text copyright © 1997 by Ann Tompert. Illustrations copyright © 1997 by Jacqueline Chwast. Reprinted by permission of Houghton Mifflin Company. All rights reserved.

p. 23, STONE SOUP by Heather Forest, illustrated by Susan Gaber. Text copyright © 1998 by Heather Forest. Illustrations © 1998 by Susan Gaber. Published by August House Publishers, Inc. Used by permission of Marian Reiner for the publisher.

p. 30, ANNIE'S GIFTS by Angela Shelf Medearis, with one illustration by Anna Rich. Published by Just Us Books. Text copyright © 1994 by Angela Shelf Medearis. Illustrations copyright © 1994 by Anna Rich.

p. 37, THE PRACTICALLY PERFECT PAJAMAS by Erik Brooks. Copyright © 2000 by Erik Brooks. Published by Winslow House International, Inc.

p. 46, THE WRECK OF THE ZEPHYR by Chris Van Allsburg. Copyright © 1983 by Chris Van Allsburg. Reprinted by permission of Houghton Mifflin Company. All rights reserved.

p. 53, BIG BUSHY MUSTACHE by Gary Soto, illustrated by Joe Cepeda. Text copyright © 1998 by Gary Soto. Illustrations copyright © 1998 by Joe Cepeda. Published by arrangement with Random House Children's Books, a division of Random House, Inc., New York, New York, U.S.A. All rights reserved.

p. 61, BRER RABBIT: THE GREAT TUG-O-WAR by John Agard, illustrated by Korky Paul. Published by The Bodley Head. Used by permission of The Random House Group Limited.

p. 68, "Horrible Harry and the Brownie Revenge" by Suzy Kline from SCHOOL'S IN! © 2001 by Suzy Kline. Reprinted by permission of the author.

p. 77, "The Astronaut and the Onion" from GLORIA RISING by Ann Cameron. Copyright © 2002 by Ann Cameron. Reprinted by permission of Farrar, Straus and Giroux, LLC.

p. 98, "Nine Gold Medals" by David Roth. Copyright © 1988 by David Roth/Maythelight Music (ASCAP) Used by permission. www.davidrothmusic.com.

p. 103, THE LIZARD AND THE SUN by Alma Flor Ada, illustrated by Felipe Dávalos. Text copyright © 1997 by Alma Flor Ada. Used by permission of Random House Children's Books, a division of Random House, Inc. Illustration copyright © 1997 by Felipe Dávalos. Used by permission of Publishers Graphics Inc.

p. 111, CHARLIE AND TESS by Martin Hall, illustrated by Catherine Walters. Text copyright © 1995 by Martin Hall. Illustrations copyright © 1995 by Catherine Walters. Originally published in Great Britain 1995 by Magi Publications, London.

p. 132, OWL MOON by Jane Yolen, illustrated by John Schoenherr. Text copyright © 1987 by Jane Yolen. Illustrations copyright © 1987 by John Schoenherr. Used by permission of Philomel books, A division of Penguin Young Readers Group (USA) Inc., 345 Hudson St., New York, NY 10014.

p. 138, From THE DREAM COLLECTOR by Troon Harrison, illustrated by Alan and Lea Daniel. Text copyright © 1999 by Troon Harrison. Illustrations copyright © 1999 by Alan and Lea Daniel. Used by permission of Kids Can Press Ltd., Toronto.

p. 151, "Eat-It-All-Elaine" from DON'T EVER CROSS A CROCODILE by Kaye Starbird. Copyright © 1961 by Kaye Starbird. Copyright renewed 1991. Used by permission of Marian Reiner.

p. 157, SAM THE ZAMBONI MAN by James Stevenson, illustrated by Harvey Stevenson. Text copyright © 1998 by James Stevenson. Illustrations copyright © 1998 by Harvey Stevenson. Reprinted by permission of the Darhansoff, Verrill, Feldman Literary Agents.

p. 165, From DONOVAN'S WORD JAR by Monalisa DeGross. Text copyright © 1994 by Monalisa DeGross. Used by permission of HarperCollins Publishers.

Illustrations
Yuri Salzman iii, vi; Teri Weidner v.

Photography
p. vii © Dennis Fagan; p. 86 © The Corcoran Gallery of Art/CORBIS; p. 88 Courtesy Library of Congress; p. 146 © Hugo Van Lawick/National Geographic Image Collection.

Contents

1 LYRIC POEM — **1**

Words Are Like Faces

By Edith Baer   Illustrated by Lori Lohstoeter

This lively poem explores the way that words help us express our thoughts and feelings.

Vocabulary:

comforting	expression
shelter	vital
fleet	versatile
glimmer	

2 REALISTIC FICTION — **7**

Gloria Who Might Be My Best Friend

By Ann Cameron   Illustrated by Ann Strugnell

A boy makes a new friend and learns how wishes come true.

Vocabulary:

tease	assume
lonely	hopeful
serious	companion
fasten	

3 SENECA LEGEND — **15**

How Rabbit Lost His Tail

Retold by Ann Tompert   Illustrated by Jacqueline Chwast

This Seneca legend explains why rabbits have short, stubby tails.

Vocabulary:

giddy	rescue
boast	resourceful
stranded	consequence
tremble	

4 FOLK TALE — **23**

Stone Soup

Retold by Heather Forest   Illustrated by Susan Gaber

Two travelers make a pot of soup with a stone and teach some villagers a lesson about sharing.

Vocabulary:

nestle	nutritious
weary	assemble
elegant	contribute
emerge	

5 REALISTIC FICTION — **30**

Annie's Gifts

By Angela Shelf Medearis   Illustrated by Anna Rich

Everyone in Annie's family can play beautiful music…except for Annie. However, Annie has gifts that are just as special.

Vocabulary:

performance	individual
carefree	artistic
talent	discord
squirm	

6 FANTASY — **37**

The Practically Perfect Pajamas

Written and illustrated by Erik Brooks

A bear who loves pajamas learns to just be himself.

Vocabulary:

vibrant	exhausted
stylish	envy
reluctant	originality
retreat	

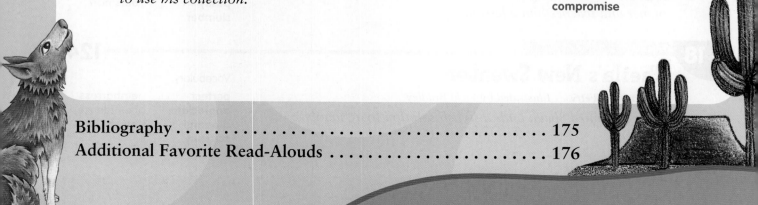

The Magic of Reading Aloud

Research Says. . .

"Read quality literature to students to build a sense of story and to develop vocabulary and comprehension."
—National Reading Panel

Many literate adults have fond memories of being read to as children. This is no coincidence. Reading research has shown that, besides being an enjoyable experience, reading aloud to children is a valuable tool in the teaching of language.

How Reading Aloud Fosters
Vocabulary Development

Children begin understanding a variety of words long before they can read them. A word that could provide a stumbling block to a child reading silently is perfectly comprehensible when the child hears the word spoken and used in context. It follows, then, that a Read-Aloud Anthology is the perfect springboard for vocabulary development.

What This Read-Aloud Does	What This Means for You
Exposes children to rich, sophisticated words used in captivating, age-appropriate stories and poems	You can add a large store of descriptive, robust words and concepts to children's vocabularies.
Provides engaging vocabulary introduction strategies after each read-aloud	You can introduce the vocabulary words in natural and memorable ways as part of your read-aloud discussion.
Encourages children to relate each vocabulary word to their own experiences	You can help children make connections with powerful words—and enjoy hearing them make the words their own!

Bringing the
Story to Life

There you are at center stage! Who, you?
A performer? Yes! Just look at your audience,
eagerly waiting for you to read them a story.
Following some simple tips will help dramatize
the performance and make it even more
satisfying and valuable for children.

Tips for Reading Aloud

Practice reading ahead of time. Reading
stories and poems aloud before reading to
children helps you read fluently, with appropriate intonations and expression.

Introduce the story. Before you begin reading, show children the illustration and ask
what they think the story will be about.

Build background. If you think there are
concepts of the selection that will be unfamiliar, provide enough background to help
children understand the reading.

Read expressively. It's difficult to overdra-
matize when reading to children. Don't be
afraid to use plenty of expression to reflect
the mood of what you are reading.

Read slowly and clearly. Listeners will be
better able to absorb and comprehend what
you are saying when they have enough time
to form mental images as they listen.

Pace your reading. The best pace is one
that fits the story event. If exciting action is
taking place, speed up a bit. To build sus-
pense, slow down and lower your voice.

Use props. Bring in or make simple props if
they will help clarify or enhance the story.

Involve your listeners. Encourage children
to make sound effects or to provide rhyming
or repeated words when a pattern has been
established.

Ask questions. As you read, ask questions
that allow listeners to make connections with
their own experiences and to stay engaged.

Listen as you read. Pay attention to children's comments during the story so you can
build on those ideas and experiences in dis-
cussions after reading.

Enjoy yourself! If you are enthusiastic about
what you are reading, children will learn that
reading is an enjoyable activity.

Research Says. . .

*. . . regular reading aloud
strengthens children's reading,
writing, and speaking skills—and
thus the entire civilizing process.*
—*The New Read-Aloud
Handbook,* Jim Trelease

Words Are Like Faces

This lively poem explores the way that words help us express our thoughts and feelings.

Vocabulary

Words From the Poem

These words appear in blue in the poem. You might wish to go over their meanings briefly before reading the poem.

comforting
Something comforting makes you feel better when you are sad or afraid.

shelter
To shelter something is to keep it from getting hurt by the sun or the weather.

fleet
A person or animal that is fleet moves fast.

glimmer
To glimmer is to shine or twinkle softly.

Words About the Poem

These words will be introduced after the poem is read, using context from the poem.

expression   **vital**   **versatile**

Getting Ready for the Read-Aloud

Show students the picture on pages 2 and 3 of the children's faces. Read the title aloud, and have students identify words that could be used to describe the facial expressions in the picture.

Read aloud the following words and have students use just their faces—no sounds—to express each emotion: *surprised, scared, sad, happy.* Have students suggest other words for the group to pantomime.

The following words occur in the poem. They can be briefly explained as you come to them in the poem: *wounding,* hurting someone's feelings; *soothing,* calming.

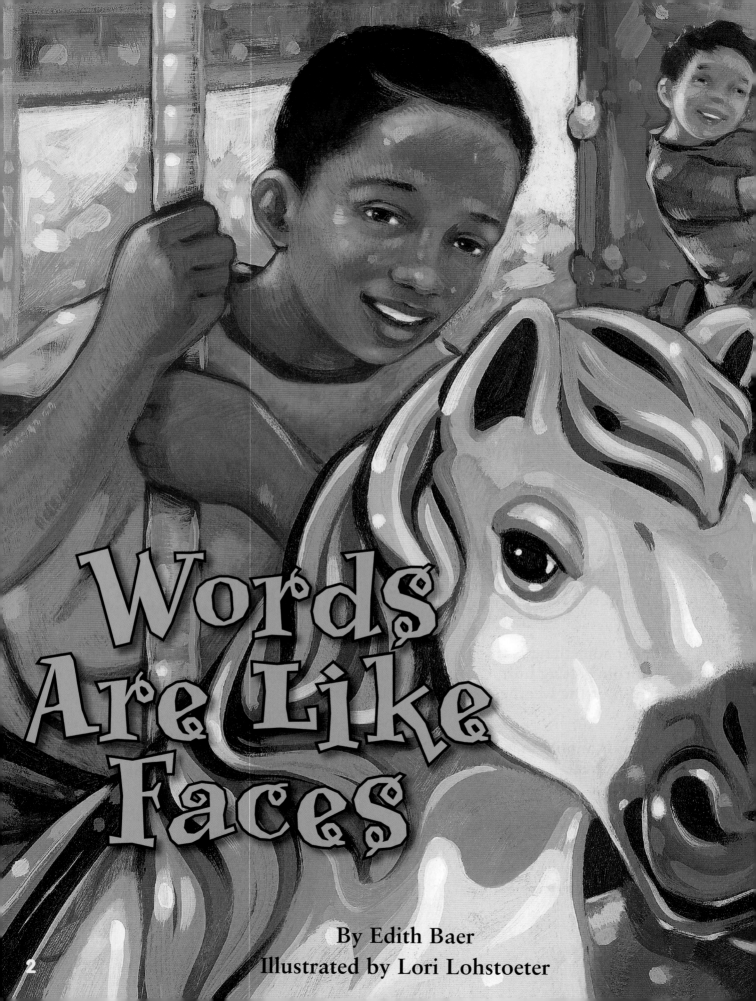

Words Are Like Faces

By Edith Baer

Illustrated by Lori Lohstoeter

2

Words can be spoken,
printed or penned,
put on a blackboard
or mailed to a friend,
passed as a secret
from one to another—
words are what people
say to each other.

Words can be plain
like a loaf of fresh bread,
comforting words
like your very own bed,
sheltering words
like the room where you play—
safe, snug and cozy,
and easy to say.

Use your voice to emphasize the poet's well-chosen words, such as *shimmer, twirl, clatter,* and *clink.* You may wish to read the entire poem once so students can appreciate its rhythm. Then read it again, pausing a few times to ask brief questions.

What are some different ways words can be?

Words can be **fleet** things,
light as a cloud,
lovely to hear
as you say them aloud—
sunlight and rainbow,
snowflake and star—
they **glimmer** and shimmer
and shine from afar.

Words can be arrows
shot from a bow,
piercing and wounding
wherever they go.
Words can be soothing
and healing instead.
Be careful with words,
for they can't be unsaid.

Why do we need to be careful with words?

Some words are like faces
we've known long before,
and some like new places
to find and explore.
Some twirl on tiptoes,
some clatter or clink,
and some sound exactly
the way you would think!

In what way are words
like faces?

Do you have favorite
words of your own?
Milkshake or magic?
Old funny bone?
Whippoorwill, daffodil,
merry-go-round?
Touch them and taste them
and try on their sound!

Words tell you're happy,
angry or sad,
make you feel better
when you feel mad,
get off your chest
what you're trying to hide—
Words tell what people
feel deep inside.

Talking About the Poem

- Why do you think the poet chose the title "Words Are Like Faces"?
- Revisit the question that begins the sixth stanza ("Do you have favorite words of your own?"). Have students share their favorite words.

Vocabulary in Action

comforting

The poem states that words can be comforting like your very own bed. Something comforting makes you feel better when you are sad or afraid.

- Ask when someone might need comforting, after losing a pet or winning first prize at a pet show. Explain why.
- Have students describe how they might comfort a pet that is afraid of thunder.

fleet

The poem says that words can be fleet things. A person or animal that is fleet moves fast.

- Ask students which animal is fleet, a cheetah or a turtle. Explain why.
- Have students show how they would move across the room in a fleet way.

shelter

Words can be sheltering like the room where you play. To shelter something is to keep it from getting hurt by the sun or the weather.

- Ask students when someone would want to find shelter, on a clear, warm day or on a cold, snowy day. Why do you think so?
- Have students show how they might shelter a favorite book in the rain.

glimmer

Some words glimmer and shimmer. To glimmer is to shine or twinkle softly.

- Ask which would glimmer, a firefly on a dark night or the bright spotlights at a circus. Why do you say that?
- Have students use glitter to create a design that glimmers.

expression

Some words are like faces. Another way to say that is to say words have expression. Your expression is the look on your face that shows what you are feeling.

- Ask students what expression their principal might have if they were to give him or her a thank-you card at the end of the school year, horrified or surprised. Explain why.
- Have students show an emotion by making a facial expression and invite others to identify the feeling expressed.

vital

Words bring thoughts and feelings to life. Another way to say that is to say words are vital. Someone or something that is vital is full of life.

- Ask which is vital, a wilting daisy or a blooming rose. Explain your answer.
- Have students draw a picture of a vital plant.

versatile

Words can be used in many different ways. Another way to say that is to say they are versatile. If someone or something is versatile, it can do many different things.

- Ask which is more versatile, a backpack or a suitcase. Why?
- Have a mini talent show in which students perform several acts at once, such as tap dancing and singing. Discuss how this illustrates *versatile*.

Gloria Who Might Be My Best Friend

In this story a boy makes a new friend and learns how wishes come true.

Vocabulary

Words From the Story

These words appear in blue in the story. You might wish to go over their meanings briefly before reading the story.

tease
When you tease someone, you try to upset them by laughing at them or making jokes about them.

lonely
Someone who is lonely feels like they don't have any friends.

serious
If someone is serious, they are thinking hard about something and are not joking around about it.

fasten
To fasten two things is to tie or somehow connect the two things together.

Words About the Story

These words will be introduced after the story is read, using context from the story.

assume   **hopeful**   **companion**

Getting Ready for the Read-Aloud

Show students the picture on page 8 of Julian doing a cartwheel while Gloria watches. Read the title aloud and tell students that Gloria has just moved into Julian's neighborhood. Julian likes her right away and hopes that they will become friends.

Julian tells how he meets Gloria and describes what they do on their first afternoon together. When Julian guesses one of Gloria's secret wishes, he is pretty sure they will be friends.

The following words occur in the story. They can be briefly explained as you come to them in the story: *squawked*, made a loud, harsh sound; *jerked*, pulled suddenly; *stiff*, hard to bend.

Gloria Who Might Be My Best Friend

By Ann Cameron
Illustrated by Ann Strugnell

Bringing the Story to Life

I f you have a girl for a friend, people find out and **tease** you. That's why I didn't want a girl for a friend—not until this summer, when I met Gloria.

It happened one afternoon when I was walking down the street by myself. My mother was visiting a friend of hers, and my little brother, Huey, was visiting a friend of his. Huey's friend is five and so I think he is too young to play with. And there aren't any kids just my age. I was walking down the street feeling **lonely**.

Use your voice to convey sincerity as Julian shares his thoughts and feelings about his new friend. Gloria's voice should communicate her maturity and confidence.

> Why was Julian feeling lonely?

A block from our house I saw a moving van in front of a brown house, and men were carrying in chairs and tables and bookcases and boxes full of I don't know what. I watched for a while, and suddenly I heard a voice right behind me. "Who are you?"

I turned around and there was a girl in a yellow dress. She looked the same age as me. She had curly hair that was braided into two pigtails with red ribbons at the ends.

"I'm Julian," I said. "Who are you?"

"I'm Gloria," she said. "I come from Newport. Do you know where Newport is?"

I wasn't sure, but I didn't tell Gloria. "It's a town on the ocean," I said.

"Right," Gloria said. "Can you turn a cartwheel?"

She turned sideways herself and did two cartwheels on the grass.

I had never tried a cartwheel before, but I tried to copy Gloria. My hands went down in the grass, my feet went up in the air, and—I fell over.

I looked at Gloria to see if she was laughing at me. If she was laughing at me, I was going to go home and forget about her.

But she just looked at me very **seriously** and said, "It takes practice," and then I liked her.

Why did Julian decide he liked Gloria?

"I know where there's a bird's nest in your yard," I said.

"Really?" Gloria said. "There weren't any trees in the yard, or any birds, where I lived before."

I showed her where a robin lives and has eggs. Gloria stood up on a branch and looked in. The eggs were small and pale blue. The mother robin squawked at us, and she and the father robin flew around our heads.

"They want us to go away," Gloria said. She got down from the branch, and we went around to the front of the house and watched the moving men carry two rugs and a mirror inside.

What made Gloria think that the birds wanted them to leave?

"Would you like to come over to my house?" I said.

"All right," Gloria said, "if it is all right with my mother." She ran in the house and asked.

It was all right, so Gloria and I went to my house, and I showed her my room and my games and my rock collection, and then I made strawberry punch and we sat at the kitchen table and drank it.

"You have a red mustache on your mouth," Gloria said.

"You have a red mustache on your mouth, too," I said.

Gloria giggled, and we licked off the mustaches with our tongues.

"I wish you'd live here a long time," I told Gloria.

Gloria said, "I wish I would too."

"I know the best way to make wishes," Gloria said.

"What's that?" I asked.

"First you make a kite. Do you know how to make one?"

"Yes," I said, "I know how." I know how to make good kites because my father taught me. We make them out of two crossed sticks and folded newspaper.

"All right," Gloria said, "that's the first part of making wishes that come true. So let's make a kite."

We went out into the garage and spread out sticks and newspaper and made a kite. I **fastened** on the kite string and went to the closet and got rags for the tail.

> Why do Gloria and Julian decide to make a kite?

"Do you have some paper and two pencils?" Gloria asked. "Because now we make the wishes."

I didn't know what she was planning, but I went in the house and got pencils and paper.

"All right," Gloria said. "Every wish you want to have come true you write on a long thin piece of paper. You don't tell me your wishes, and I don't tell you mine. If you tell, your wishes don't come true. Also, if you look at the other person's wishes, your wishes don't come true."

Gloria sat down on the garage floor and started writing her wishes. I wanted to see what they were—but I went to the other side of the garage and wrote my own wishes instead. I wrote:

1. I wish I could see the catalog cats.
2. I wish the fig tree would be the tallest in town.
3. I wish I'd be a great soccer player.
4. I wish I could ride in an airplane.
5. I wish Gloria would stay here and be my best friend.

> Why does Julian go to the other side of the garage to write his wishes?

I folded my five wishes in my fist and went over to Gloria.

"How many wishes did you make?" Gloria asked.

"Five," I said. "How many did you make?"

"Two," Gloria said.

I wondered what they were.

"Now we put the wishes on the tail of the kite," Gloria said. "Every time we tie one piece of rag on the tail, we fasten a wish in the knot. You can put yours in first."

What is Gloria's plan for making wishes? Do you think it will work? Why or why not?

I fastened mine in, and then Gloria fastened in hers, and we carried the kite into the yard.

"You hold the tail," I told Gloria, "and I'll pull."

We ran through the back yard with the kite, passed the garden and the fig tree, and went into the open field beyond our yard.

The kite started to rise. The tail jerked heavily like a long white snake. In a minute the kite passed the roof of my house and was climbing toward the sun.

We stood in the open field, looking up at it. I was wishing I would get my wishes.

"I know it's going to work!" Gloria said.

"How do you know?"

"When we take the kite down," Gloria told me, "There shouldn't be one wish in the tail. When the wind takes all your wishes, that's when you know it's going to work."

How do you know your wishes will come true?

The kite stayed up for a long time. We both held the string. The kite looked like a tiny black spot in the sun, and my neck got stiff from looking at it.

"Shall we pull it in?" I asked.

"All right," Gloria said.

We drew the string in more and more until, like a tired bird, the kite fell at our feet.

We looked at the tail. All our wishes were gone. Probably they were still flying higher and higher in the wind.

Maybe I would see the catalog cats and get to be a good soccer player and have a ride in an airplane and the tallest fig tree in town. And Gloria would be my best friend.

Why does Julian think that his wishes might come true?

"Gloria," I said, "did you wish we would be friends?"

"You're not supposed to ask me that!" Gloria said.

"I'm sorry," I answered. But inside I was smiling. I guessed one thing Gloria wished for. I was pretty sure we would be friends.

Talking About the Story

- Ask students to explain how they can tell that Julian and Gloria might become best friends.
- Ask students to tell about some things they like to do with a friend. Encourage them to describe things about themselves that make them a good friend.

Vocabulary in Action

tease

In the story Julian claims that if a boy has a girl for a friend, people will tease him. When you tease someone, you try to upset them by laughing at them or making jokes about them.

- Ask who would be more likely to tease someone, a school principal or a classmate. Explain your answer.
- Have students tell how it feels to be teased.

serious

Gloria looks at Julian very seriously when he tries to do a cartwheel. If someone is serious, they are thinking hard about something and are not joking around about it.

- Ask in which place you are more likely to be serious, on the playground or at the doctor's office. Why?
- Have pairs of students act out situations in which one person is silly and the other is serious.

lonely

Julian feels lonely because no kids his age live nearby. Someone who is lonely feels like they don't have any friends.

- Ask which would make someone lonely, eating lunch with a friend or missing a friend who is on vacation. Why do you think so?
- Have students describe moments in which someone might feel lonely.

fasten

Julian fastens string to the kite that he and Gloria make. To fasten two things is to tie or somehow connect the two things together.

- Ask which you fasten in a car, a seatbelt or a steering wheel. Explain why.
- Ask a student to fasten paper strips to form a chain.

assume

Julian believes that he will be made fun of if he has a friend who is a girl. He assumes others will tease him. When you assume something, you believe it is true, even when it might not be.

- Ask students which thing they would assume to be true, a newspaper article or a rumor. Why?
- Call on two students to act out a scene in which one student wrongly assumes something about the other, such as that he or she likes sports, doesn't like school, etc.

companion

Gloria and Julian play together the day they meet. They become companions. A companion is someone you spend time with or do things with.

- Ask who makes a better companion on a walk, a dog or a turtle. Explain why.
- Ask students to explain what they like about their companions and why.

hopeful

Julian thinks that Gloria will be his friend. In other words, Julian is hopeful that he and Gloria will become friends. If you are hopeful, you believe that something good will happen.

- Ask which would be hopeful, worrying about a test or expecting to do well. Explain.
- Have students write a hopeful message to cheer up someone.

How Rabbit Lost His Tail

This Seneca legend explains why rabbits have short, stubby tails.

Vocabulary

Words From the Story

These words appear in blue in the story. You might wish to go over their meanings briefly before reading the story.

giddy
When you are giddy, you are so happy that you start to act silly.

boast
When you boast about something, you talk about it in a way that is so proud that it is like showing off.

stranded
When you are stranded somewhere, you are left behind with no way to leave.

tremble
To tremble means to shake all over because you are very scared or very angry.

Words About the Story

These words will be introduced after the story is read, using context from the story.

rescue   resourceful   consequence

Getting Ready for the Read-Aloud

Show students the picture on page 16 of Rabbit with his long, flowing tail. Read the title aloud and tell students that long ago people made up this story to explain why rabbits have such short, stubby tails.

Ask students if they have ever wondered why animals look the way they do. Explain that animals have features that help them survive. Discuss the giraffe's long neck, the cat's sharp claws, and the baby deer's spotted fur. Tell students that long ago, people told stories to explain things in nature, such as why animals have certain features.

The following words occur in the story. They can be briefly explained as you come to them in the story: *chortled,* laughed happily; *wafted,* carried gently through the air; *wailed,* cried in pain.

How Rabbit Lost His Tail

A Seneca legend retold by Ann Tompert
Illustrated by Jacqueline Chwast

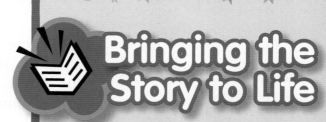

Along time ago when the world was young, Rabbit's tail was not short and stubby like it is now. It was once long and flowing like Squirrel's.

It all began one moonlit night when Rabbit was in a grove of willow trees nibbling some twigs from a raspberry bush. Thoughts of sweet juicy clover and other tasty tidbits filled his head, making him quite **giddy**.

He began to run around a willow tree.

Faster and faster he ran.

"No one can run faster than me," he **boasted**. As he raced round and round, dark clouds drifted over the moon. Soon snow floated down. Rabbit began to sing.

Let it snow, snow, snow.

Watch me go, go, go.

Toe and heel, heel and toe

Round and round I go, go, go.

Now, it seemed to Rabbit that the faster he raced around the willow tree, the faster and thicker the snow fell. "Look at me!" he chortled. "Look at me! I'm making it snow!"

He was so pleased with himself that he ran and ran until he was too tired to take another step.

He was bursting with pride as he glanced about and saw that all the bushes and small trees were now covered by a blanket of snow. "I've made enough snow for now," he declared. "I'll just take a little rest before I make any more."

Use a voice that portrays each character's feelings. For example, Rabbit is elated in the beginning but fearful when he becomes stranded. Porcupine is unsympathetic to Rabbit's plight. Also be guided by verbs such as *chortled, wailed,* and *boasted*.

Why was Rabbit so pleased with himself?

Because he had never learned to climb, he looked for a willow tree with a branch close enough to the snow for him to jump onto. He soon found just the right tree, settled himself on a branch, wrapped himself with his tail, and fell asleep.

How was Rabbit able to climb into the willow tree so easily?

Rabbit was so tired that he slept for a very long time. While he was sleeping the weather warmed.

The snow melted and grass, sweet clover, and other green plants sprouted. When Rabbit awoke, he found himself **stranded** high above the ground.

Why was Rabbit high above the ground when he awoke?

"Oh, dear!" he wailed. "What am I going to do?"

He was trying to figure out how he could get down when Porcupine came walking along. She stopped under Rabbit's tree to eat the sweet clover growing there.

"Help! Help!" cried Rabbit.

Porcupine looked up.

"What's the matter?" she asked.

"I want to get down from here," said Rabbit.

"Climb down, silly," said Porcupine.

"I don't know how," said Rabbit.

"Too bad," said Porcupine. And she went on eating.

A gentle spring breeze wafted the smell of sweet clover up toward Rabbit. He sniffed.

"I'm so hungry," he wailed.

"Climb down or starve," said Porcupine.

"Like it or not, I'll have to climb down," Rabbit told himself.

***

Why does Rabbit want so badly to climb down from the tree?

Holding his breath, he put one foot toward the trunk of the tree. His body wobbled. He froze.

Just then, along came Badger.

"Help! Help! Help!" Rabbit cried.

"What's the matter?" asked Badger, looking up at Rabbit.

"He can't climb down," snorted Porcupine. "Imagine!"

"I never learned how," said Rabbit.

"How did you get up there then? Fly?"

"No. No, No!" cried Rabbit, shaking his head.

He told Badger about running and making snow.

"But when I woke up," he said, "the snow had melted and I was stranded. I'd climb down if I knew how."

"Are you afraid?" asked Badger.

"What? Me, afraid?" cried Rabbit.

"Climbing trees is not my specialty," said Badger.

"Digging is. I'll just dig a hole under your tree. It will sink lower and lower as I make the hole deeper and deeper. In no time you'll be close to the ground."

***

How does Badger plan to help Rabbit?

Badger soon disappeared into the earth in a shower of dirt.

Badger was still digging when Beaver came along.

"What are you doing?" he called.

"I'm helping Rabbit," he said, pointing. "I'm digging a hole under this tree so it will sink down."

"I can't climb down," said Rabbit. "I never learned how."

"I'll bet you're just afraid," said Beaver.

"Whatever gave you that idea?" cried Rabbit, standing on his hind feet. "I'll show you who's afraid!" He inched one foot along the branch, swayed, sat down, and froze.

"He's afraid to climb down," declared Porcupine, tossing her head.

"Why don't I just cut the tree down?" said Beaver. He started to gnaw on the trunk. The tree **trembled**.

How does Beaver plan to help Rabbit?

"Stop! Stop! Stop!" cried Rabbit.

"What's the matter?" asked Beaver.

"If this tree falls, I could get hurt," said Rabbit.

Just then Squirrel came by.

"What's going on?" she asked.

"Rabbit wants to get down from this tree," said Beaver.

"But he's afraid to climb down," snorted Porcupine.

"I'm hungry," wailed Rabbit.

"Why don't you jump?" asked Squirrel.

"That's it!" exclaimed Beaver. "Why didn't I think of that? All you have to do is jump!"

"Jump!" cried Rabbit. "I can't jump that far!"

"There's nothing to it," said Squirrel.

"Let me show you."

Why is Squirrel so confident about jumping out of the tree?

In a twinkling she was up the trunk of the tree and out on Rabbit's limb. Then, with a flash of her tail, she sailed down to the ground.

"Your turn," she called up to Rabbit.

"I can't!" wailed Rabbit.

But he knew he had to. "If I don't jump, I'll starve," he said to himself.

Then, taking a deep breath, he squeezed his eyes shut and leaped.

Seconds later he landed, turning a somersault.

"Your tail!" cried Porcupine, pointing.

Rabbit looked up. There was his tail, waving in the breeze. It was caught in the crotch of the tree where he had been sitting.

What happens to Rabbit's tail when he jumps from the tree?

"Oh, dear!" cried Rabbit. "Will somebody please get my tail?"

"I have to fix a hole in my dam," said Beaver.

"I'm on my way to visit Woodchuck," said Badger.

"Go get your own tail," said Porcupine.

"You look just fine without it," said Squirrel.

And the four hurried away.

From that day forth, all members of Rabbit's tribe have had little stubby tails. And every spring the tiny white tails we see hanging on willow trees remind us of how it all happened.

Talking About the Story

- Ask students to explain how Rabbit got caught in the tree, how each animal tried to help, and what happened in the end.
- Ask students if they have ever been stuck somewhere. Have them describe how they became stuck and how they got free.

Vocabulary in Action

giddy

In the story the thought of clover made Rabbit giddy. If you are giddy, you are so happy that you start to act silly.

- Ask students what might make them giddy, taking out the trash or going to their favorite amusement park. Explain your answer.
- Have students imitate a giddy person.

tremble

The willow tree trembled when Beaver started to gnaw on its trunk. To tremble means to shake all over because you are very scared or very angry.

- Ask which would make you tremble, facing an angry bear or facing a playful kitten. Why do you say that?
- Ask students to imitate someone trembling.

boast

Rabbit boasted that no one can run faster than he can. When you boast about something, you talk about it in a way that is so proud it seems like showing off.

- Ask students which they would boast about, losing their lunch money or scoring the winning goal in a soccer game. Why?
- Have a student pretend to boast.

stranded

Rabbit found himself stranded in a tree. If you are stranded somewhere, you are left behind with no way to leave.

- Ask in which situation someone would be stranded, in a car with an empty gas tank or in a car that is stopped in traffic. Why?
- Ask a student to act out being stranded in a boat on a lake.

rescue

Rabbit asked his friends to help him get down from the tree. In other words, he asked to be rescued. To rescue someone is to save them from something bad happening.

- Ask who would need to be rescued, a person locked outside his home when the oven is on or a person moving into a new house. Why do you think so?
- Ask two students to act out rescuing a kitten stuck in a very tall box.

resourceful

Squirrel was clever. He found a way to solve Rabbit's problem. Another way to say that is to say Squirrel was resourceful. Someone who is resourceful is good at solving problems.

- Ask which person is more resourceful, someone who reuses plastic shopping bags or someone who buys plastic bags at the store. Give a reason for your answer.
- Ask students to act out a resourceful way of bringing a lot of books back to the library.

consequence

Rabbit jumped from the tree and lost his tail. Rabbit losing his tail was a consequence of jumping out of the tree. A consequence is what happens because you did or did not do something.

- Ask which might be a consequence of brushing your teeth, clean teeth or a set of braces. Why?
- Ask a student to act out a consequence of missing the bus.

Stone Soup

In this folk tale two travelers make a pot of soup with a stone and teach some villagers a lesson about sharing.

Vocabulary

Words From the Story

These words appear in blue in the story. You might wish to go over their meanings briefly before reading the story.

nestle
If you nestle something, you hold it against yourself softly.

weary
If you are weary, you are very tired.

elegant
Something elegant is beautiful and fancy.

emerge
To emerge means to come out from behind or under something and into view.

nutritious
If a food is nutritious, it has things in it that will make your body healthy.

Words About the Story

These words will be introduced after the story is read, using context from the story.

assemble   **contribute**

Getting Ready for the Read-Aloud

Show students the picture on pages 24 and 25 of the man throwing a stone into a pot of soup. Read the title aloud and tell students that the story explains how to make a good pot of soup with a stone and one other special ingredient.

Explain that sometimes people are unwilling to share what they have with those in need. In this story two travelers help some villagers realize the good that comes from sharing what you have—no matter how small.

The following words occur in the story. They can be briefly explained as you come to them in the story: *tattered*, torn into shreds; *tartly*, sharply; *glee*, joy.

Stone Soup

A European tale retold by Heather Forest
Illustrated by Susan Gaber

There was once a comfortable little village **nestled** in the mountains. The people who lived there had more than enough to keep themselves content.

One day two travelers came along. Their coats were tattered. Their hats were torn. Their dusty shoes had holes in their soles.

Hungry and tired, one traveler said to the other, "Surely someone here can spare a bit of food."

Bringing the Story to Life

Use your voice and facial expressions to convey the villagers' attitudes toward the travelers. Emphasize the rhythm of the repeated text that occurs throughout the story.

They knocked boldly on a door. It creaked open and a woman asked, "What do you want?"

"Please," said one of the weary travelers, "we are hungry. Do you care? Will you share? Do you have any food?"

The woman squinted her eyes and tartly replied, "No!" She quickly slammed the door shut.

The travelers walked a little farther down the road and knocked on another door. A young boy answered. His chocolate brown eyes were sweet.

"Good day," he said shyly. "What do you want?"

"Please," said one of the travelers, "we are hungry. Do you care? Will you share? Do you have any food?"

The boy replied, "There is no food here" and closed the door.

The travelers wandered **wearily** through the village, knocking on every door. But everywhere they heard, "I don't care. I won't share. There is no food!"

> What happens every time the travelers ask for food?

They sat to rest beside a well. One traveler sighed and clutched his empty belly. He said, "If there is really no food in this **elegant** little village, then the people who live here are in greater need than we are. We should make them our special soup."

The two travelers climbed up on the edge of the well and shouted, "We are master cooks! If anyone in this town has a big black pot, we will make the most delicious soup anyone ever tasted!"

A door slowly opened. A round man **emerged** carrying a gigantic black pot. "I love to eat!" he said. "Here's a pot. Let me see what two master cooks can do with it."

"Watch and see!" said one traveler with glee.

The travelers filled the pot with cold water and built a fire. Soon the flames licked the sides of the pot and billows of steam rose into the air. Curious people began to gather. "What is happening?" the townspeople asked.

"We are making an unusual soup," said one of the travelers. "It requires a special ingredient. I am certain we will find it in this town."

All the eyes in the crowd watched as one of the travelers reached down and picked up an ordinary stone. He tossed it into the pot with a splash. "We're making Stone Soup!" he said.

"It will be **nutritious**, delicious, incredible, and edible! But it would taste better," he paused and sighed, "if we only had a carrot."

"Where would we find a carrot in this town?" the other traveler asked. "We knocked on every door and everywhere we heard, 'I don't care. I won't share. There is no food!'"

"Then perhaps we cannot make the delicious soup after all," they both announced with a sad shrug of their shoulders, and began to turn away.

A child timidly raised her hand and said, "Wait! I might have a small carrot."

"Excellent!" shouted the travelers. "Bring what you've got! Put it in the pot! We're making Stone Soup!"

"This soup would taste even better if we had a potato," they added.

A deep voice in the back of the crowd called out, "I have a potato."

> What happens when the travelers ask for ingredients for the soup?

"Wonderful!" shouted the travelers. "Bring what you've got! Put it in the pot! We're making Stone Soup!"

"It would taste better still," they said, "if we had just a few more ingredients."

"Perhaps," said one villager, "I could bring a green bean."

"Well," said another, "if you are going to bring a green bean, I will bring a kernel of corn."

"I shall not be outdone," cried another. "I will bring an egg noodle!"

One by one, voices announced, "I will bring a slice of celery!" "I will bring a pinch of pepper." "I can bring a sprig of parsley!" "I might have a tiny turnip!"

"Well, why are you waiting?" cried the travelers. "Bring what you've got. Put it in the pot. We're making Stone Soup!"

Everyone in the town ran home to bring one small thing to put in the pot. Food flew through the air and landed with splashes in the growing soup. Soon the huge pot was full and simmering. A wonderful smell drifted through the air.

The smell was so tempting, people brought out bowls, spoons, chairs, and tables. They placed hearty loaves of bread, chunks of cheese, and bowls of fruit on the tablecloths.

Everyone came to taste the soup and marveled at the flavor. "It's amazing!" said one woman.

"These two travelers made such a delicious soup out of a stone."

"Out of a stone," said the travelers with a grin, "and a special ingredient...*sharing.*"

As the travelers left the town they said, "If anyone ever wants to make this soup again, just remember the recipe.

Bring what you've got.
Put it in the pot.
Every bit counts,
from the largest to the least.
Together we can celebrate
a Stone Soup feast!"

How did the townspeople change when the travelers started making stone soup? Why do you think that happened?

Talking About the Story

- Ask students to explain what happened in the village the day that two tired, hungry travelers appeared.

- Ask students to recall a time when they shared something with others. What happened? Is it always easy to share? Why or why not?

Vocabulary in Action

nestle

In the story the travelers visit a village that is nestled in the mountains. If you nestle something, you hold it against yourself softly.

- Ask students which they might nestle, a puppy or a porcupine. Why do you think so?
- Have a student show how to nestle a stuffed animal.

weary

The travelers wander wearily through the village. If you are weary, you are very tired.

- Ask students which might make someone weary, not getting enough sleep or not getting enough attention. Why?
- Call on a student to walk wearily around the classroom.

elegant

One of the travelers describes the village as elegant. Something elegant is beautiful and fancy.

- Ask which clothes are elegant, denim blue jeans or a silk dress. Explain why.
- Have students draw a picture of an elegant home.

emerge

In the story a round man emerges from his house carrying a gigantic pot. To emerge means to come out from behind or under something and into view.

- Ask which an animal could emerge from, an open field or a dark cave. Explain what you mean.
- Have students hide in the classroom and then emerge one by one as you call their names.

nutritious

One of the travelers declares that the soup will be nutritious. If a food is nutritious, it has things in it that will make your body healthy.

- Ask which would be more nutritious, an apple or a candy bar. Why?
- Ask students to draw pictures of nutritious foods.

Words About the Story

assemble

A cook must put together many different ingredients to make a tasty soup. In other words, the cook must assemble the ingredients. To assemble something means to put all of the different parts of it together.

- Ask which you might assemble, a jigsaw puzzle or a live grizzly bear. Explain your answer.
- Call on a student to assemble a board game so that it is ready to play.

contribute

Many villagers bring vegetables to throw into the pot of soup. Another way to say this is to say that the villagers contribute to the soup. If you contribute to something, like an event, you give or do something to help make it a success.

- Ask which you might contribute to, a soup kitchen for the homeless or a fast food restaurant. Why do you say that?
- Ask students to bring something to contribute to a classroom collection.

ANNIE'S GIFTS

Everyone in Annie's family can play beautiful music...except for Annie. However, Annie has gifts that are just as special.

Vocabulary

Words From the Story

These words appear in blue in the story. You might wish to go over their meanings briefly before reading the story.

performance
You give a performance when you do something like sing, dance, play an instrument, or speak in front of an audience.

carefree
A carefree person acts happy and does not have any worries.

talent
Talent is a natural ability to do something well.

squirm
When you squirm, you wiggle from side to side because you are uncomfortable or nervous.

Words About the Story

These words will be introduced after the story is read, using context from the story.

individual   artistic   discord

Getting Ready for the Read-Aloud

Invite students to look at the picture of Annie on page 31. Read aloud the title, and tell students that in this story, a gift means something special that a person can do well. Ask if they can guess what Annie's gifts might be from looking at the picture.

Explain that different people have different gifts. Point out some of the gifts of students in your class. For example, you might mention one student's gift for helping people and another's ability to run fast.

The following words occur in the story. You may explain them briefly as you encounter them in the story: *carousel*, a merry-go-round; *recorder*, a kind of a musical instrument that you blow into like a flute; *diesel truck*, a type of truck that has a noisy engine.

ANNIE'S GIFTS

By Angela Shelf Medearis
Illustrated by Anna Rich

Once there lived a family that loved music. Every morning the children, Lee, Patty, and Annie, turned on some music. The floors trembled as they stomped their feet to the loud bass beat. Soon they were moving down the street to catch the school bus.

After the children left for school, Momma would turn on the radio. Momma swayed with the sweet rhythm as she sipped her coffee.

Every night, after the children were in bed, Daddy would say, "Come on honey! Let's go once around the floor." Then he and Momma slow danced to the soulful, blues music he loved.

Lee loved music so much that he joined his school band. Annie thought Lee looked wonderful in his uniform with the shiny brass buttons. Lee's music sounded like the circus. When he swung into a song on the trumpet, Annie tapped her feet and clapped her hands.

Patty was a wonderful musician, too. When Patty played the piano it made Annie think of pretty colors, soft rain, and springtime flowers. Patty also had a lovely singing voice. When company came, she would entertain the guests.

Imitate the sounds used to describe Annie's playing, such as squawking chickens and screeching alley cats (or ask students to supply those sound effects). Also, use your voice to highlight the disappointment and frustration Annie feels about not being able to play music.

What did everyone in Annie's family have in common?

"Wonderful, just wonderful," the guests would sigh and clap their hands after Patty's **performance**. Annie decided that she wanted to play an instrument, too.

One day, Annie's school music teacher, Mrs. Mason, passed out instruments to the class. She gave Annie a recorder.

The class practiced a group song for months. Everyone played their part perfectly, everyone, except Annie. When Annie played, the recorder squeaked and squawked like chickens at feeding time.

"I don't think the recorder is the instrument for you," Mrs. Mason said.

Why did Mrs. Mason say she didn't think the recorder was the instrument for Annie?

"I guess you're right," Annie said. "Maybe I can play the cello."

"Let's give it a try," Mrs. Mason said. "I'll show you how to play it."

When Mrs. Mason played the cello, it sounded warm and **carefree**, like carousel music. Annie tried and tried, but when she played the cello, it always sounded like a chorus of screeching alley cats.

"Oh," Mrs. Mason sighed and rubbed her ears. "Annie, darling, I just don't think this is the instrument for you. How would you like to make a banner and some posters announcing our program?"

"Okay," said Annie. She was disappointed, but she did love to draw. Annie drew while everyone else practiced.

That evening, Annie picked up Lee's trumpet and tried to play it. Her playing sounded like an elephant with a bad cold. Lee begged her to stop. Annie's feelings were hurt, but she put the trumpet away.

"I wish I could find an instrument to play," Annie told her mother.

"Cheer up!" Momma said. "We're going to get a new piano and everyone is going to take piano lessons!"

What kind of piano player do you think Annie will be?

Soon, a beautiful, new piano was delivered to Annie's house. The piano was made of shiny, brown mahogany. Annie peeked under the piano lid while Patty played a song. "Melody Maker" was written in beautiful gold letters.

That week, all three children started piano lessons with Mrs. Kelly. After every lesson, Mrs. Kelly gave them new sheet music to practice.

Patty and Lee did very well. Mrs. Kelly always told them how **talented** they were.

Oh, but when Annie played the piano, Mrs. Kelly's smile turned into a frown. The low notes sounded like a diesel truck honking its horn, the middle ones like croaking frogs, and the high notes sobbed like a crying baby.

Once, Annie tried to sing and play the piano for her parents' guests. Her performance made everyone **squirm** in their chairs. Annie was so embarrassed that she went up to her room and cried. She couldn't play the recorder or the cello. She couldn't play the piano or sing or play the trumpet. Annie had never felt so sad in her life.

Why was Annie sad?

Sometimes, when Annie was sad, she liked to write poetry to make herself feel better. She decided to write a poem about music.

I love to hear music play.

I practice hard every day.

But even though I try and try,

the sounds I play

make people laugh and cry.

That night, Annie put her poem on Daddy's pillow. Then she went to sleep.

In the morning, Daddy and Momma had a long talk with Annie.

"I just can't seem to do anything right," Annie sighed.

Why did Annie think that she couldn't do anything right?

"Yes, you can," Daddy said. "There are lots of things you can do."

"Really, Daddy?" Annie asked.

"Of course," Momma said. "Not everyone can play the piano and sing like Patty. Not everyone can play the trumpet like Lee. That's his special gift. And not everyone can write poetry and draw beautiful pictures the way you can."

"I didn't think about it that way," Annie said. "I can't sing or play an instrument well, but I can do *a lot* of other things."

Now, if you should pass by Annie's house, you might hear Patty singing and playing on the piano. Perhaps you'll hear Lee playing his trumpet. And sometimes, if you stop and listen very, very closely, you might hear Annie playing…**her radio!**

Annie plays loud, finger-popping music when she feels like laughing and drawing pictures. She plays soft, sweet music when she writes her poems. She can play any kind of music she likes on her radio.

She still can't play the piano or sing like Patty, and she still can't play the trumpet like Lee.

But now Annie has found she's happiest when drawing her pictures and writing poetry. Because art and writing are Annie's gifts.

Talking About the Story

- Ask students to tell how Annie felt at the beginning, middle, and end of the story. Have them explain what happened in each part to make her feelings change.
- Invite students to tell about gifts they have and describe how they discovered that they have these gifts.

Vocabulary in Action

performance

In the story Annie's sister gives a performance. You give a performance when you do something like sing, dance, play an instrument, or speak in front of an audience.

- Ask which is a performance, someone telling a joke on stage or eating a snack. Why?
- Ask students to give a performance with an imaginary musical instrument.

squirm

Annie's piano playing was so bad that it made everyone squirm in their chairs. When you squirm, you wiggle from side to side because you are uncomfortable or nervous.

- Ask which could make someone squirm, getting ready to sing to lots of people or watching television. Why?
- Have students squirm in their chairs.

talent

Annie's family has musical talent. Talent is the natural ability to do something well.

- Ask which is an example of a talent, sneezing when you have a cold or being able to spell lots of words. Explain.
- Invite students to share their talents with the class.

carefree

The teacher's music is carefree. A carefree person acts happy and does not have any worries.

- Ask students which might make them feel more carefree, playing on a playground or taking care of a sick pet. Explain your answer.
- Have a student walk around the classroom in a carefree way.

Words About the Story

individual

Annie has talents unlike her family's. She is an individual. Sometimes the word *individual* is used to describe a person who does not try to imitate others.

- Which would make a person an individual, liking the color blue or liking ketchup on cereal? Why?
- Do a simple dance step and have students imitate it. Then ask them to create and demonstrate their own individual dance steps.

artistic

Annie could make posters, banners, and beautiful pictures. She is artistic. When someone is artistic, it means that they are very good at drawing, painting, or making beautiful things.

- Ask whether a person would need artistic talent to make a clay statue of a cat or to buy one. Explain what you mean.
- Ask students to point to something that was made by an artistic person.

discord

Annie's music sounded awful. The sound she made was discord. Discord occurs when things, like musical notes, are out of tune or disagree with one another.

- Ask students if they would be more likely to hear discord on the radio or during a beginners' band class. Why?
- Lead students in singing a familiar song. Then repeat it with discordant notes.

The Practically Perfect Pajamas

In this story a bear who loves pajamas learns to just be himself.

Vocabulary

Words From the Story

These words appear in blue in the story. You might wish to go over their meanings briefly before reading the story.

vibrant
Something that is vibrant is very bright and colorful.

stylish
A stylish person wears clothes that are in fashion and make them look good.

reluctant
Reluctant means you are not sure you want to do something.

retreat
When you retreat, you move quickly away from someone or something.

exhausted
If you are exhausted, you are so tired that you have no energy left.

Words About the Story

These words will be introduced after the story is read, using context from the story.

envy   originality

Getting Ready for the Read-Aloud

Invite students to look at the picture of Percy the bear on page 39. Read aloud the title and point out that Percy is wearing his favorite pajamas.

Explain that Percy is a polar bear. Tell students that polar bears live in the Arctic where it is very, very cold. Their white fur coats help them blend into their snowy surroundings. Help students locate the Arctic on a map or globe.

It might be helpful to explain briefly the following words that may be unfamiliar to students: *practically,* another word for almost; *flannel,* a soft, warm kind of cloth; *stain-resistant,* something that does not get spots on it when something is spilled.

The Practically Perfect Pajamas

Written and illustrated by
Erik Brooks

ercy was a polar bear who loved his footed pajamas more than anything else in the world. The pajamas were a **vibrant** red with bright yellow stars. They were perfect for reading the morning paper, ideal when enjoying an afternoon snack, and a cozy necessity for a good night's sleep.

His pajamas protected his beautiful white coat from icicles between his toes, from spills when he was clumsy, and from too much shivering while he was taking a nap.

Unfortunately, Percy's pj's were only practically perfect. Not everyone liked his pajamas as much as he did.

"Hey, fancy pants," said one bear.

Bringing the Story to Life

Modulate your voice to Percy's changing moods, such as resignation at giving up his pj's and loneliness when he is teased by the other bears. Aurora's dialogue should have an admiring, supportive tone.

"Where's the circus?" said another.

"Why can't you be more like the rest of us?" shouted a third.

The bears teased him endlessly, and the other animals kept their distance.

Even the Arctic foxes, who were well known for following polar bears, never followed Percy.

"A bear dressed like *that?*" they chuckled. "We don't want anything to do with him."

Percy was all alone—or so he thought.

Aurora was one Arctic fox who couldn't stay away. She loved Percy's **stylish** pajamas, and admired that he was brave enough to be different. "I don't care what anyone else thinks," she said. "There is nothing silly about Percy or his pj's."

One morning Percy decided that he'd had enough.

"My pajamas are great," he sighed, "but this teasing has got to stop. Practically perfect just isn't good enough."

Reluctantly he boxed up his pajamas and put them away forever. "Perhaps now the others will like me," he said to himself and headed outside.

> Why did Percy decide to put away his pajamas forever?

Aurora was surprised when Percy appeared without his pj's. "What can he be up to?" she said to herself. "I'd better keep an eye on him today."

A lifetime in footed pajamas had not prepared Percy for his new journey into the Arctic. He waded through several icy pools of melting snow. "This isn't so b-b-b-a-ad," he said, shivering, even though his tender feet were suffering. "Ouch. Ooooh," Percy yelped. The soft furry pads and hairs between his toes froze quickly to the ice.

"Hey, can anybody help me?" Percy called out. "My feet are stuck!" Several bears glanced in his direction, but no one came to his rescue. Instead, they simply shook their heads and wandered away.

"I wouldn't be here right now if I had my pj's," Percy whimpered. After several painful tries, he wrenched his feet loose and **retreated** to his den.

While his paws were thawing, Percy tried to cheer up over a late morning snack. He was feeling much better, until he accidentally bumped his cocoa. The thick chocolate syrup erupted from his mug and landed right in his lap, leaving a giant stain on his beautiful white coat.

"How can this be happening?" he said. "This is supposed to be a perfect day."

Percy grabbed a brush and scrubbed his fur, trying to get clean. It was impossible work. The scrubbing only spread the cocoa deeper into his coat. **Exhausted**, he slumped to the floor.

"I think I need a good nap," he said.

Without his pajamas, however, sleeping was impossible, too. No matter what—left side, right side, upside, or downside—Percy could not get comfortable.

What troubles did Percy have when he stopped wearing his pj's?

"Maybe some fresh air will do me good," he said aloud.

As he lumbered toward the door, Percy paused in front of a mirror. He hardly recognized himself. His fur was stained and matted, and his restless nap had left large, puffy bags under both eyes. Out of habit, he looked around for his favorite flannel pajamas.

"No," he muttered, shaking his head. "I don't need them."

The Arctic sun was as high and hot as it could be, so Percy stepped outside to warm himself. This time he moved slowly and carefully. "How does everybody manage?" he wondered. "This isn't very easy."

Percy soon realized that getting your feet stuck in the snow was very common. He also noticed several other bears with large dirty stains on their fur and big, puffy bags under their eyes.

"Everyone looks miserable," he thought. "Maybe all bears should wear pajamas." He quickly remembered, however, that his pajamas were only practically perfect. "I may be cold, dirty and tired," he said, "but at least now no one is laughing at me."

With renewed hope, Percy ran into a large crowd of bears roughhousing at the edge of the ice.

What did Percy hope would happen?

"Hey, Percy," one of the older bears shouted. "Where are your star-studded, flannel-footed peee-jays? Did ya lose 'em?"

"No!" said Percy. "I decided not to wear them today."

"My, oh my," mocked the oldest. "Percy's finally gonna act like a real bear."

"But I am…," Percy hesitated. "I *am* a real bear!"

"At least you're finally acting like one," said the others. "Come along and play with us today."

Percy smiled. "Perfect," he thought. "I'm part of the group." He bounced back and forth, grinning from ear to ear. "What are we playing?" he asked. "Freeze-tag? Leapfrog? Duck-duck-goose?"

The bears circled quietly, and Percy waited. Deep in the crowd, someone whispered softly, "1…2…3…Go!"

Suddenly Percy felt a powerful shove from behind and went tumbling toward the icy Arctic water. He barely had time to brace himself before the bitter cold seized him from nose to tail.

Stunned, Percy quickly gathered himself and swam to the surface. The other bears were laughing and pointing.

"Pretty fun game, eh, Percy?" said the biggest bear.

"Where are your waterproof pj's when you really need them?"

Percy was crushed.

> What happened when Percy tried to play with the other bears?

"I guess they just don't like me," he said, sinking into the slushy ice and dragging himself ashore. Never in his life had he been so cold and wet and lonely. All he could think about was the warmth and comfort of something friendly and familiar.

Looking up, Percy realized that he wasn't alone.

"Go on, fox, laugh away," he said. "I must be quite a funny sight."

But Aurora didn't laugh. "Hello, Percy," she said. "My name is Aurora. You don't know me, but I've been watching you for a long time. I miss seeing you in your splendid pajamas."

"You do?" Percy answered.

"Yes, of course," Aurora chimed. "The other bears are too dull. You always seem so happy in your pj's. I can't imagine why you'd go anywhere without them. They fit you perfectly!"

"Well, thank you," said Percy. "I thought the others might like me better if I didn't wear them."

"Oh, Percy," said Aurora kindly. "That's nonsense. They obviously don't know what they're missing. Follow me, I've got a great idea." The two of them headed toward Percy's den.

After discussing Aurora's plan on the walk home, Percy made an even bigger decision than the one that he'd made that morning.

> What do you think the plan could be?

They rushed inside and got right to work. Together, Percy and Aurora dug through mounds of flannel pajamas and sorted out the very best that Percy had to offer. Soon they had moved all of his pj's outside.

As they shook them out and folded them neatly on the snow, a small crowd gathered around.

"My goodness, stain resistant? These are very nice," said one bear.

"And these colors...Mmm, Mm. Very flattering," exclaimed a second.

"Someone has been living right!" whistled yet another bear. The sign that Percy and Aurora made said it all.

A day spent in these perfect pj's

is far better than a day spent without them.

Even if you do look a bit silly sometimes.

Slowly but surely, the bears helped themselves. As Percy slipped once again into his own favorite pair, he knew Aurora was right.

Warm, happy, and wrapped in footed flannels, the two new friends looked proudly at the scene.

"So much for practically perfect," said Percy. "These pj's are positively perfect!"

Talking About the Story

- Encourage students to tell in their own words what Percy's problem was and how he and Aurora solved it.
- Invite students to tell about things that are special to them even if no one else thinks so.

Vocabulary in Action

vibrant

In the story Percy's favorite pj's were vibrant red. Something that is vibrant is very bright and colorful.

- Ask which is vibrant, the color of an orange or the color of soil. Tell why.
- Ask one student to pick out something in the room that has a vibrant color. Other students should ask questions and guess what the object might be.

reluctant

Percy was reluctant to put away his favorite pj's. Reluctant means you are not sure you want to do something.

- Ask which you would be more reluctant to touch, a soft kitten or a rotten peach. Why?
- Have students show how they would act if they were reluctant to touch a slimy toad.

stylish

Aurora thought Percy's pj's were stylish. A stylish person wears clothes that are in fashion and make them look good.

- Ask which might look more stylish, an old pair of jeans they have outgrown or a new pair of pants that fit just right. Explain your answer.
- Have students describe the most stylish outfit they have seen.

retreat

After a difficult morning, Percy retreated to his home. When you retreat, you move quickly away from someone or something.

- Ask which would be more likely to make people retreat, being caught in a rainstorm or receiving a nice gift. Explain why.
- Ask volunteers to come to the front of the room and then retreat to their seats.

exhausted

Percy was exhausted after he tried to clean his fur. If you are exhausted, you are so tired that you have no energy left.

- Ask which might make you more exhausted, watching a movie or riding a bike for an hour. Why do you think so?
- Have students act out being exhausted after running a race.

Words About the Story

envy

The other bears wished they had fancy pj's like Percy's. They envied Percy. You envy someone when you wish that you had what they have.

- Which would you envy, a person who has lots of friends or has lots of chores to do? Explain.
- Ask a volunteer to act like someone who envies what another has.

originality

Percy was unlike the other animals because he wore pajamas. In other words, Percy's actions showed originality. Something has originality if it is the first of its kind or if it is unlike anything else.

- Ask which shows originality, memorizing a poem or writing your own poem. Why?
- Ask students to point to something in the classroom that shows originality.

The Wreck of the Zephyr

A mysterious old man tells the tale of a boy who learned a very unusual way to sail a boat.

Vocabulary

Words From the Story

These words appear in blue in the story. You might wish to go over their meanings briefly before reading the story.

anchor
When you anchor something, you attach it to something else so that it won't move.

ominous
Something is ominous if it makes you think that something bad or unpleasant is about to happen.

blustery
A blustery wind is a strong wind that changes direction quickly.

astonished
If you are astonished, something has surprised you so much that you feel shocked.

treacherous
If something or some place is treacherous, it is very dangerous.

Words About the Story

These words will be introduced after the story is read, using context from the story.

defiant   **strive**

Getting Ready for the Read-Aloud

Ask students to look at the sailboat pictured on page 47. Read aloud the title and tell students that *Zephyr* is the name of the boat. Point out that *zephyr* is also another word for a gentle breeze.

Explain that a sailboat moves when the wind catches in the sails and pushes the boat along. Even an experienced sailor might have trouble steering one of these boats in bad weather.

Quickly review the meanings of the following words, which may be unfamiliar to students: *rigging,* the ropes and chains that hold up and control sails on a sailboat; *boom,* the long pole on a sailboat that holds the sail; *reef,* a mound of rock or shells near the edge of the water; *tiller,* the part of a sailboat used to steer it.

The Wreck of the Zephyr

Written and illustrated by Chris Van Allsburg

Once, while traveling along the seashore, I stopped at a small fishing village. After eating lunch, I decided to take a walk. I followed a path out of the village, uphill to some cliffs high above the sea. At the edge of these cliffs was a most unusual sight—the wreck of a small sailboat.

An old man was sitting among the broken timbers, smoking a pipe. He seemed to be reading my mind when he said, "Odd, isn't it?"

"Yes," I answered. "How did it get here?"

"Waves carried it up during a storm."

"Really?" I said. "It doesn't seem the waves could ever get that high."

Bringing the Story to Life

Establish a persona for the man telling the story. Use a voice that is a bit old and mysterious. When you finish reading, slowly stand and limp away, pretending to use a cane.

> What is unusual about the wrecked sailboat?

The old man smiled. "Well, there is another story." He invited me to have a seat and listen to his strange tale.

"In our village, years ago," he said, "there was a boy who could sail a boat better than any man in the harbor. He could find a breeze over the flattest sea. When dark clouds kept other boats at **anchor**, the boy would sail out, ready to prove to the villagers, to the sea itself, how great a sailor he was.

"One morning, under an **ominous** sky, he prepared to take his boat, the *Zephyr*, out to sea. A fisherman warned the boy to stay in port. Already a strong wind was blowing. 'I'm not afraid,' the boy said, 'because I'm the greatest sailor there is.' The fisherman pointed to a sea gull gliding overhead. 'There's the only sailor who can go out on a day like this.' The boy just laughed as he hoisted his sails into a **blustery** wind.

> How did the boy feel about himself and his skills as a sailor?

"The wind whistled in the rigging as the *Zephyr* pounded her way through the water. The sky grew black and the waves rose up like mountains. The boy struggled to keep his boat from going over. Suddenly a gust of wind caught the sail. The boom swung around and hit the boy's head. He fell to the cockpit floor and did not move.

"When the boy opened his eyes, he found himself lying on a beach. The *Zephyr* rested behind him, carried there by the storm. The boat was far from the water's edge. The tide would not carry it back to sea. The boy set out to look for help.

"He walked for a long time and was surprised that he didn't recognize the shoreline. He climbed a hill, expecting to see something familiar, but what he saw instead was a strange and unbelievable sight. Before him were two boats, sailing high above the water. **Astonished**, he watched them glide by. Then a third sailed past, towing the *Zephyr*. The boats entered a bay that was bordered by a large village. There they left the *Zephyr*.

What strange sight did the boy see?

"The boy made his way down to the harbor, to the dock where his boat was tied. He met a sailor who smiled when he saw the boy. Pointing to the *Zephyr* he asked, 'Yours?' The boy nodded. The sailor said they almost never saw strangers on their island. It was surrounded by a **treacherous** reef. The *Zephyr* must have been carried over the reef by the storm. He told the boy that, later, they would take him and the *Zephyr* back over the reef. But the boy said he would not leave until he learned to sail above the waves. The sailor told him it took years to learn to sail like that. 'Besides,' he said, 'the *Zephyr* does not have the right sails.' The boy insisted. He pleaded with the sailor.

"Finally the sailor said he would try to teach him if the boy promised to leave the next morning. The boy agreed. The sailor went to a shed and got a new set of sails.

"All afternoon they sailed back and forth across the bay. Sometimes the sailor took the tiller, and the boat would magically begin to lift out the water. But when the boy tried, he could not catch the wind that made boats fly.

What did the boy want to do? Was he successful?

"When the sun went down they went back to the harbor. They dropped anchor and a fisherman rowed them to shore. 'In the morning,' the sailor said, 'we'll put your own sails back on the *Zephyr* and send you home.' He took the boy to his house, and the sailor's wife fed them oyster stew.

"After dinner the sailor played the concertina. He sang a song about a man named Samuel Blue, who, long ago, tried to sail his boat over land and crashed:

'For the wind o'er land's ne'er steady nor true,
an' all men that sail there'll meet Samuel Blue.'

"When he was done with his song, the sailor sent the boy to bed. But the boy could not sleep. He knew he could fly his boat if he had another chance. He waited until the sailor and his wife were asleep, then he quietly dressed and went to the harbor. As he rowed out to the *Zephyr*, the boy felt the light evening wind grow stronger and colder.

What do you think the boy will do?

"Under a full moon, he sailed the *Zephyr* into the bay. He tried to remember everything the sailor had told him. He tried to feel the wind pulling his boat forward, lifting it up. Then, suddenly, the boy felt the *Zephyr* begin to shake. The sound of the water rushing past the hull grew louder. The air filled with spray as the boat sliced through the waves. The bow slowly began to lift. Higher and higher the *Zephyr* rose out of the water, then finally broke free. The sound of rushing water stopped. There was only the sound of wind in the sails. The *Zephyr* was flying.

"Using the stars to guide him, the boy set a course for home. The wind blew very hard, churning the sea below. But that did not matter to the *Zephyr* as she glided through the night sky. When clouds blocked the boy's view of the stars, he trimmed the sails and climbed higher. Surely the men of the island never dared fly so high. Now the boy was certain he was truly the greatest sailor of all.

"He steered well. Before the night was over, he saw the moonlit spire of the church at the edge of his village. As he drew closer to land, an idea took hold of him. He would sail over the village and ring the *Zephyr's* bell. Then everyone would see him and know that he was the greatest sailor. He flew over the tree-topped cliffs of the shore, but as he reached the church the *Zephyr* began to fall.

Why did the boy want to sail over the village and ring the Zephyr's bell?

"The wind had shifted. The boy pulled as hard as he could on the tiller, but it did no good. The wind shifted again. He steered for the open sea, but the trees at the cliff's edge stood between him and the water. At first there was just the rustle of leaves brushing the hull. Then the air was filled with the sound of breaking branches and ripping sails. The boat fell to the ground. And here she sits today."

"A remarkable tale," I said, as the old man stopped to relight his pipe. "What happened to the boy?"

"He broke his leg that night. Of course, no one believed his story about flying boats. It was easier for them to believe that he was lost in the storm and thrown up here by the waves." The old man laughed.

Do you believe the man's story? Why or why not?

"No sir, the boy never amounted to much. People thought he was crazy. He just took odd jobs around the harbor. Most of the time he was out sailing, searching for that island and a new set of sails."

A light breeze blew through the trees. The old man looked up. "Wind coming," he said. "I've got some sailing to do." He picked up a cane, and I watched as he limped slowly toward the harbor.

Talking About the Story

- Ask students to retell in their own words the adventure of the young sailor.
- Invite students to tell how they think it would feel to be on a sailing ship that could fly. Do they think they would enjoy the experience? Why or why not?

Vocabulary in Action

anchor

In the story the boy went sailing during storms when other boats were anchored. When you anchor something, you attach it to something else so that it won't move.

- Which could anchor a tablecloth on a picnic table, a beach ball or a rock? Why?
- Have students try different ways of anchoring a balloon to a desk.

blustery

The wind was blustery when the boy got ready to sail. A blustery wind is a strong wind that changes direction quickly.

- Ask which would be better to do on a blustery day, play indoors or have a picnic. Explain why.
- Invite students to act out trying to walk against a blustery wind.

ominous

The sky looked ominous on a stormy morning. Something is ominous if it makes you think that something bad or unpleasant is about to happen.

- Ask whether an ominous sky would be clear or cloudy. Why is that?
- Have students describe other things that could be ominous, such as sounds.

astonished

The boy was astonished when he saw the flying boats. If you are astonished, something has surprised you so much that you feel shocked.

- Ask students which would be more likely to make them feel astonished, a tiger in their yard or a phone call from a friend. Why?
- Have students act out a situation in which they are astonished.

treacherous

A treacherous reef surrounded the island. If something or some place is treacherous, it is very dangerous.

- Which would be a treacherous thing to meet in the woods, a bear or a rabbit? Why?
- Have students draw pictures of treacherous places, such as a steep waterfall, a rocky canyon, or a dark cave.

defiant

A fisherman warned the boy not to go out in the storm, but the boy didn't obey. The boy was defiant. If you are defiant, you refuse to obey others.

- Ask which are defiant, friends sharing a treat or bike riders without helmets. Explain why.
- Give students a direction and have them act out the response of a defiant child.

strive

The boy wanted to show he was the best sailor. He was striving to prove that he was the best. If you strive for something, you work very hard to get it.

- Ask whether a person would strive to be a good student or to eat a sandwich. Why?
- Ask students to act out striving to climb to the top of a mountain.

BIG BUSHY MUSTACHE

In this story a boy who is in a hurry to grow up gets a very special gift from his father.

Vocabulary

Words From the Story

These words appear in blue in the story. You might wish to go over their meanings briefly before reading the story.

victory
A victory is winning a struggle in a war or competition.

smear
When you smear something, you spread a layer of it over something else.

creation
A creation is something that someone has made using their skills and creativity.

disguise
A disguise is something you wear to make you look like someone or something else.

Words About the Story

These words will be introduced after the story is read, using context from the story.

admire   **resemble**   **pretend**

Getting Ready for the Read-Aloud

Ask students to look at the picture on page 55 of the boy walking down the street. Have students notice what is unusual about the boy. Then read the title aloud. Invite students to guess why the boy has a mustache.

Invite any students who know people who have mustaches to describe them. Explain that sometimes men grow mustaches because they like how they look. Some men grow mustaches so they will look older.

Provide a brief introduction of some words that may be new to students: *sarape,* a colorful blanket used as a cape in Mexico; *sombrero,* a Mexican hat with a very wide brim; *bigote,* the Spanish word for mustache.

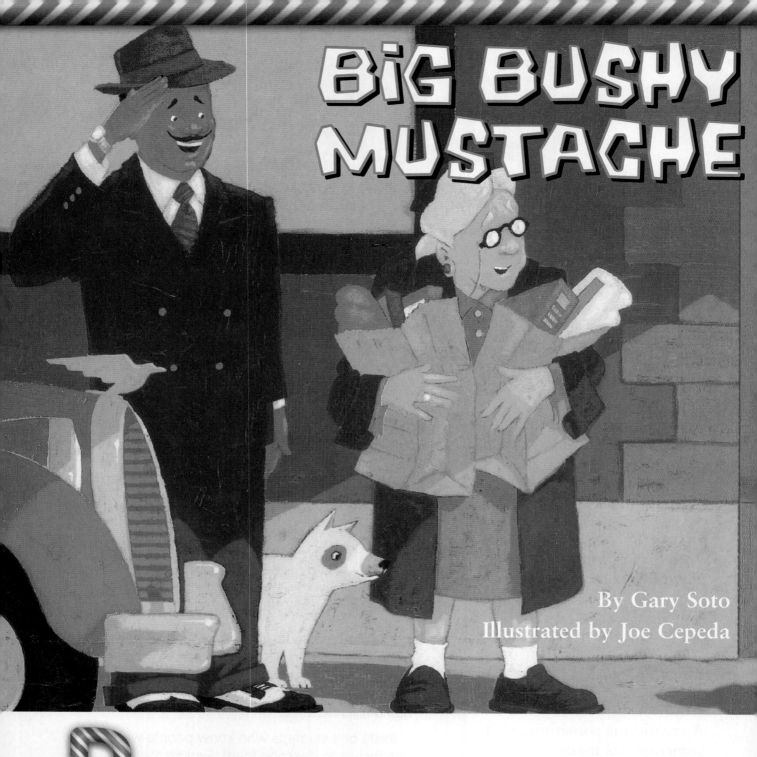

BIG BUSHY MUSTACHE

By Gary Soto
Illustrated by Joe Cepeda

People always said Ricky looked just like his mother.

"He has beautiful eyes, exactly like yours, Rosa!" said Mrs. Sanchez, the crossing guard, as his mother took him to school one morning.

"Thanks!" Ricky's mother shouted, and turned a big smile on him. "Have a good day, *mi'jo* (MEE hoh)." Then she gave him a kiss.

Bringing the Story to Life

Before you read the story, cut out a mustache from black paper. At the point in the story where Ricky gets a fake mustache in school, put it up to your lip. Continue to use the paper mustache at key points in the story.

Ricky went into school frowning. He was a boy. Why didn't people say he looked like his father?

That morning his teacher, Mrs. Cortez, brought out a large box from the closet and set it on her desk. She took out a hat and a *sarape* (sah RAH peh). She took out a wooden sword and raised it toward the ceiling.

"Class, for our next unit we're going to do a play about *Cinco de Mayo* (SEEN koh deh MY oh). That's a holiday that celebrates the Mexican **victory** over the French army."

Mrs. Cortez looked around the room. Her eyes settled on Ricky. "Ricky, do you want to carry the sword?"

Ricky shook his head no.

"Do you want to wear this white shirt?" she asked.

Again Ricky shook his head no. And he shook his head to the *sombrero,* the captain's hat, the purple cape, the tiny Mexican flag.

But when Mrs. Cortez took out a big, bushy mustache, something clicked. This time Ricky nodded yes.

> Why do you think Ricky wanted the mustache?

For the rest of the day, the class practiced their parts. Some of the children played Mexican soldiers. Some of the children played French soldiers.

All the while, Ricky played with his mustache. It tickled his lip. It made him feel tough.

When school was over, Mrs. Cortez told the class to leave the costumes in their desks.

Ricky took off his mustache. But instead of leaving it behind, he put it in his pocket. He wanted to take it home. He wanted to surprise his father when he got home from work. *Maybe Mami will take a picture of us,* he thought. *We could stand next to each other in front of our new car.*

After Ricky left the school, he pressed the mustache back onto his lip. He felt grown-up.

A man on the street called out, "Hello, soldier."

Ricky passed a woman carrying groceries. She said, "What a handsome young man."

He passed a kindergartner, who said, "Mister, would you help me tie my shoes?"

Ricky laughed and ran home. He climbed the wooden steps, pushed open the door, and rushed into the kitchen, where his mother was peeling apples.

How did the mustache change the way Ricky felt about himself?

"*Hola, Mami!* (OH lah MAH mee)" he said. "I'm hungry."

He looked up and waited for her to say something about his big, bushy mustache.

But she only smiled and handed him a slice of apple.

"*Mi'jo*, wash your hands and help me with the apples," she said. Ricky's smile disappeared. Didn't she notice?

"Look, Mami. Isn't my *bigote* (bee GOH teh) great?" he said, tugging at her apron. His mother looked at him.

"Bigote? What are you talking about?"

"This one," he said. He touched his lip, but the mustache was gone! He felt around his face. It was not on his cheek. It was not on his chin. He looked down to the floor, but it wasn't there, either.

I must have lost it on the way home, Ricky thought. Without saying anything, he ran out the front door.

What do you think Ricky will do?

He retraced his steps, eyes wide open. He dug through a pile of raked leaves. He parted the tall grass that grew along a fence. He looked in the street, between parked cars, and in flower beds.

He jumped with hope when he saw a black thing. But when he bent over to pick it up, he discovered that it was a squashed crayon.

Ricky sat on the curb and cried. The mustache was gone.

When he got home, Ricky told his mother what had happened. She wiped her hands on a dish towel and hugged him.

At dinner, he wanted to tell Papi too, but the words would not come out. They were stuck in his throat.

He watched his father's big, bushy mustache move up and down when he chewed.

Under his breath, Ricky whispered, "Mustache," but his father didn't hear. He talked about his work.

After dinner, Ricky went to his bedroom. With a black crayon, he colored a sheet of paper and then cut it into the shape of a mustache. He taped it to his mouth and stood before the mirror. But it didn't look real. He tore it off, crumpled it, and tossed it on the floor.

In the closet, Ricky found a can of black shoe polish. He looked in the mirror and **smeared** a line above his lip, but it was too flat, not thick and bushy at all.

Finally, he dug out a pair of old shoes. The strings were black. He cut them in short strips and bound them together with a rubber band. He held the **creation** above his lip. It looked like a black mop. And smelled like old socks.

> What did Ricky try to do when he went to his bedroom after dinner? What were the results?

That night, after he put on his pajamas, Ricky went into the living room, where his father was listening to the radio.

"Papi, I lost my mustache...*mi bigote.*"

His father laughed. "What mustache?"

Ricky climbed into his father's lap and told him everything. His father smiled and told him a story about a hen that tried to become a swan. It was a good story, but it still didn't solve his problem. Tomorrow he would have to face Mrs. Cortez.

The next morning, Ricky got out of bed slowly. He dressed slowly. He combed his hair slowly. At breakfast, he chewed his cereal slowly. He raised his eyes slowly when his father came into the kitchen. "*Buenos días* (BWEH nohs DEE ahs)," he greeted Ricky.

Then Ricky's mother came into the kitchen. "*Mi'jo*, I have a surprise for you," she said.

Mami held out a closed fist and let it open like a flower. Sitting in her palm was a mustache. It was big and bushy.

"You found it!" Ricky shouted happily.

"Well, yes and no," Mami said as she poured herself a cup of coffee.

Ricky pressed the new mustache to his lip. He ate his cereal, and the mustache moved up and down, just like his father's.

But something was different about his father's smile. His lip looked funny. Ricky jumped up and threw his arms around Papi's neck. His mustache was gone!

Why was Papi's mustache gone?

"*Gracias, Papi* (GRAH see ahs PAH pee)! Thank you!" he cried.

"That's okay," Papi told him. "But next time listen to your teacher."

Then Papi touched his son's hair softly. "And, hey, now I look just like you!"

Ricky grinned a mile wide.

When Ricky walked to school, he carried the mustache not on his lip, but safely in his pocket.

It wasn't just a bushy **disguise** anymore, but a gift from his papi.

Talking About the Story

- Ask students to tell how Ricky's feelings changed from the beginning to the end of the story. Have them explain what happened to make his feelings change.
- Encourage students to tell about a time a family member or friend helped them to solve a problem.

Vocabulary in Action

victory

In the story, the class was planning to celebrate Mexico's victory over the French army. A victory is winning a struggle in a war or competition.

- Which would be a victory, winning an art contest or making a greeting card for your grandmother? Explain your answer.
- Have two students act out running a race across the front of the classroom. Ask the class to identify who had a victory.

disguise

Ricky wore a mustache as a disguise. A disguise is something you wear to make you look like someone or something else.

- Ask which would be a disguise, a funny pair of glasses or a pair of scissors. Why?
- Have each student quickly draw an animal face on a sheet of paper and hold it up to their face as a disguise.

smear

Ricky smeared shoe polish on his lip to make a mustache. When you smear something, you spread a layer of it over something else.

- Ask which you would smear on your legs, suntan lotion or a pair of pants. Why do you think so?
- Invite students to act out smearing jelly on toast.

creation

Ricky's creations were pretend mustaches he made from paper and shoestrings. A creation is something that someone has made using their skills and creativity.

- Ask where someone is more likely to find a creation, in a tent or in an art museum. Explain why.
- Ask students to act out making a creation from clay.

Words About the Story

admire

Ricky wanted to be like his father. Another way to say this is that Ricky admired his father. When you admire someone, you look up to that person and want to be like them. When you admire something, you like looking at it.

- Ask students if they would be more likely to admire a garden hose or a flower. Why do you say that?
- Ask students to describe someone they admire.

resemble

People told Ricky that he looked like his mother. Another way to say that is to say Ricky resembled his mother. If you resemble someone, you look like that person.

- Ask whether someone would be more likely to resemble a person or an animal. Explain your answer.
- Ask students to point to the person in the class that they come closest to resembling.

pretend

Ricky made believe his fake mustache was real. Another way to say that is that he pretended it was real. When you pretend, you act like something that isn't real actually is.

- Ask which is pretending, children playing that they are astronauts or a boy practicing the piano. Why?
- Ask each student to pretend to be an animal.

Brer Rabbit The Great Tug-o-War

In this story a clever rabbit teaches his two bragging friends a lesson about friendship.

Vocabulary

Words From the Story

These words appear in blue in the story. You might wish to go over their meanings briefly before reading the story.

heave
When you throw something heavy as hard as you can, you heave it.

bout
A bout is a contest.

horizon
The horizon is the line far away where the earth and sky seem to meet.

dawdle
When you dawdle, you take longer to do something than is really necessary.

sprawl
To sprawl is to lie or sit with your arms and legs all spread out.

Words About the Story

These words will be introduced after the story is read, using context from the story.

defeat   obvious

Getting Ready for the Read-Aloud

Show students the picture on pages 62 and 63 of Rhino and Hippo struggling in their tug-of-war. Read the title aloud, and ask students to describe a tug-of-war.

Explain that Brer Rabbit, the main character in this story, is featured in many folk tales and stories. He is often portrayed as a clever trickster. In this story Brer Rabbit tries to teach his friends a lesson by playing a trick on them.

The following word occurs in the story. It can be briefly explained as you come to it in the story: *mite*, something tiny.

Brer Rabbit
The Great Tug-o-War

By John Agard

Illustrated by Korky Paul

He was brainy. He was bouncy. He was bob-tailed. He was Brer Rabbit. And he didn't have many muscles to talk about.

But Rhino and Hippo were always talking about their muscles.

Always boasting about who was stronger, and who was tougher, and who was badder.

"I can lift that mountain with one **heave** of my horn," Rhino said.

"I can lift that river with one shrug of my shoulder," Hippo said.

"And I can balance a forest on my hip," Rhino said.

"And I can balance this whole island on my mouth," Hippo said.

One day Rhino and Hippo were having another **bout** of boasting when Brer Rabbit stepped in:

"Lifting and balancing is easy to do. But I can outpull the two of you. I'm talking tug-o-war, gentlemen."

"Tug-o-what?" Rhino and Hippo asked.

"Tug-o-war," said Brer Rabbit. "Imagine a long rope. At one end there's you or you. At the other end there's me. We pull and pull to see who will outpull who. Bet my bob tail against your horn. Bet my whiskers against your waddle. I'll tire you guys out."

What does Brer Rabbit want Rhino and Hippo to do?

Here we go again, thought Rhino and Hippo. More hippity-hoppity jokes from the silly rabbit.

But Brer Rabbit was never more serious.

"You think you're the mighty. You think I'm the mite. Well, tomorrow, the mighty will meet the mite in tug-o-war," he declared.

Rhino and Hippo said, "Right."

They wanted to get rid of Brer Rabbit and go on with their boasting.

"I can balance the **horizon** on the tip of my horn," Rhino said.

"I can balance the milky way on the tip of my mouth," Hippo said.

"And I can lift the lightning with my left leg," Rhino said.

"And I can lift the thunder with my big toe," Hippo said.

Why did Rhino and Hippo agree to Brer Rabbit's plan?

Bright and early the next morning Brer Rabbit returned with a long rope tied around his waist.

The rope went swish-swish-swish through the thick grass and **dawdled** behind him like an eternal tail.

And though he was struggling with the rope he shouted in a loud voice for all to hear: "Wonderful day for tug-o-war to begin. I'm going to pull that Hippo out of his skin."

Hippo was sniffing the swampy morning when Brer Rabbit showed up with his rope.

"Here, Hippo," said Brer Rabbit. "Take this end. I'm off to the far side of the island.

Hold tight. Wait till you feel me pull. Then start pulling with all your might."

> What do you think Brer Rabbit is going to do?

What Hippo didn't know was that Brer Rabbit had planned to meet Rhino on the far side of the island.

"Without a heave or a huff, I'll pull that Rhino till he's puffed," called Brer Rabbit into the empty sky.

When Brer Rabbit got there, Rhino was already waiting.

"Sorry to be late," Brer Rabbit said. "A rope takes its time."

And he repeated word for word what he had told Hippo: "Here, Rhino, take this end. I'm off to the far side of the island. Hold tight. Wait till you feel me pull. Then start pulling with all your might."

With a bob and a strut Brer Rabbit disappeared into the bushes. He gave the rope a quick pull on both sides.

This was the moment Rhino and Hippo had been waiting for, yet it seemed to take them by surprise.

Neither Rhino nor Hippo was prepared for such a tugging. Rhino had to use his horn to stop himself from slipping.

Hippo had to dig in his heels to stop himself from sliding.

They pulled and pulled until they were both falling backwards.

Rhino pulling Hippo, Hippo pulling Rhino, and neither had a clue who was pulling whom. Maybe this Brer Rabbit was stronger than they thought.

"I'll lift that little lettuce nibbler and send him **sprawling** on his whiskers!" said Rhino.

"I'll pull that brat of a bunny till his floppy ears go all giddy!" said Hippo.

Suddenly, the rope burst in the twinkling of a snap. And Rhino and Hippo bundled bottomwards with a mighty splash.

> What was the outcome of the tug-of-war?

All the monkeys and all the birds—who Brer Rabbit called his friends in high places—were laughing from their tree-top seats.

Among the bushes, Brer Rabbit was cracking up, till all over he tweaked and twitched.

Rhino and Hippo had to laugh. They knew they had been tricked. They each felt like a thorough fool and a dope.

But from that day on they became friends. And Brer Rabbit would remind them that "Friendship is longer than rope."

Talking About the Story

- Ask students to describe how Brer Rabbit tricked Rhino and Hippo into having a tug-of-war with each other.
- Ask students if they've ever seen boasting lead to an unexpected situation. What happened?

Vocabulary in Action

heave

In the story, Rhino boasts that he can lift a mountain with a heave of his horn. When you throw something heavy as hard as you can, you heave it.

- Ask which a person could probably heave, a mountain or tree branch. Why?
- Call on a student to act out heaving something heavy.

horizon

Rhino says he can balance the horizon on the tip of his horn. The horizon is the line far away where the earth and sky seem to meet.

- Are you more likely to see a horizon in the city or at the seashore? Explain why.
- Have students draw a picture of the horizon.

bout

Rhino and Hippo are involved in a bout of boasting. A bout is a contest.

- Ask which you would do in a bout, help someone learn a skill or try to beat them in performing the skill. Explain your answer.
- Have pairs of students act out an imaginary bout, such as a tug-of-war.

dawdle

The rope that Brer Rabbit is carrying dawdles behind him like a long tail. When you dawdle, you take longer to do something than is really necessary.

- Ask which would make someone dawdle on the way to school, a rainstorm or a sunny day. Why?
- Ask students to show how someone would dawdle while crossing the room.

sprawl

The upset Rhino says he will pull hard on the rope and send Brer Rabbit sprawling. To sprawl is to lie or sit with your arms and legs all spread out.

- Are you sprawled out when you are sitting at your desk at school, or when you are lying on the floor at home watching TV? Tell how you know.
- Have students sprawl in their chairs.

Words About the Story

defeat

Rhino and Hippo argue a lot about who is strongest. Each one is sure he could defeat Brer Rabbit in a tug-of-war. To defeat someone is to beat that person in a contest.

- Ask which a team might do following a defeat, celebrate or practice harder. Why?
- Ask students to show how they would act if they had just been defeated in a race.

obvious

Rhino and Hippo know that they are stronger than Brer Rabbit. It is obvious that they will win any contest that Brer Rabbit plans. Something obvious is easy to see or understand.

- Ask which is obvious, a friend is wearing a red shirt or a friend's favorite color is red.
- Ask students to point to obvious places in the classroom where they could go to read quietly.

HORRIBLE HARRY
and the
Brownie Revenge

In this story Harry gets revenge for an unfair trick and ends up having an adventure at the same time.

Vocabulary

Words From the Story

These words appear in blue in the story. You might wish to go over their meanings briefly before reading the story.

spiral
Something that is spiral winds around and around, with each curve either above or outside the one before it.

ceremony
A ceremony is an event during which special things are done or said.

abrupt
If something is abrupt, it is very quick and sometimes unpleasant.

stale
When something is stale, it is no longer fresh.

Words About the Story

These words will be introduced after the story is read, using context from the story.

persuade   disgust   deceive

Getting Ready for the Read-Aloud

Show students the picture on page 69 of Harry unwrapping the brownies he made. Read aloud the title and point out that the words *horrible* and *revenge* tell you that in the story Harry may do some things that cause trouble.

Explain to students that sometimes when people get hurt, they try to get even with the person who harmed them by hurting that person in return. In other words, they try to get revenge.

The following word occurs in the story. It can be briefly explained as you come to it in the story: *revenge*, an act that involves punishing or harming someone who has hurt you.

HORRIBLE HARRY
and the
Brownie Revenge

By Suzy Kline

Illustrated by Jennifer Emery

Bringing the Story to Life

M y name is Doug. I write stories about my best friend, Harry. He loves creepy things, slimy things, and anything horrible.

He doesn't like being bugged. If he is, he won't tattle. He'll get revenge! Revenge can be a knuckle noogie on your head, a tickle attack, or ice down your back. Once he even made someone say, "I love girls!" twice.

Use a gruff voice to reflect Harry's reputation for being horrible. Your facial expressions can help convey the excitement of the ride down the slide and Sidney's disgust at the special ingredient in Harry's brownies.

Does Harry sound horrible to you? Why or why not?

The first week of third grade, Harry added a new one to his list: brownie revenge.

It all started during morning conversation when everyone was talking about the new playscape.

"I saw it as soon as I got off the bus!" Mary exclaimed. "It looks like a castle sitting on a big rubber mat. Did anyone see the slide?"

"I did! It's cool," Sidney replied. "It looks like a curly noodle with a tunnel!"

"It's a **spiral** slide," Mary snapped.

"There are monkey bars and rope swings, too!" Ida added.

Even shy Song Lee was talking about the new playscape. "I love slides! I went on the big one at Mountainside Park twenty times this summer!" Then she blushed.

"How come the playscape is roped off with yellow ribbon?" I asked.

"Yeah!" Sidney replied. "When can we go on it?"

"Well," Miss Mackle replied. "There is a special **ceremony** planned for next Monday. The mayor will be here to cut the ribbon. You'll have to wait."

"But that's a whole week!" Mary complained.

"That's not fair!" Sidney groaned.

Song Lee got a sad look.

"I'm sorry, class," the teacher replied. "The mayor is still on vacation and won't return until then."

Why can't the kids use the playscape yet? What trouble do you think this might cause?

Harry didn't care. He **abruptly** changed the subject. "I made brownies all by myself," he bragged.

Mary raised her eyebrows.

The teacher smiled. "Why, Harry, I didn't know you liked to cook."

"I didn't, either," Harry replied. "But I did a lot of it this summer. See?"

Everyone watched Harry unfold the tinfoil. "One brownie is crunchy and the other is creamy."

"Kind of burnt, aren't they?" Sidney said.

Harry shot Sidney a look. "I doubled the chocolate."

Now Sidney started to drool. "Can I have one?"

"The creamy one is for…"

I looked at Harry. I was hoping he'd give it to me.

"For…Song Lee," Harry said with a toothy smile.

I should have known. Harry's been in love with her since kindergarten.

Song Lee took the brownie and smiled. "Thank you, Harry," she said softly.

Sidney fumed. "Can I have the other one?" he begged. "Please?"

"No," Harry said. "I'm saving it."

What did Harry brag to his classmates about?

At two o'clock, we went outside for recess. Everyone walked over to the playscape and touched the yellow ribbon. The spiral slide shone in the sun.

"It feels like summer," Mary said. "It's so hot!"

"Too hot for kickball," Dexter groaned.

"Want to look for ladybugs in the grass?" Ida suggested.

Lots of kids followed her over to the lawn.

Harry took his jacket off right away and laid it on the pavement. Then he set his brownie that was still wrapped in tinfoil on top.

"Hey, Harry the canary," Sidney said skipping by, "can I have that brownie?"

"You're starting to bug me!" Harry warned.

"Please, pretty please?" Sidney nagged.

"For the hundredth time, no!"

What do you think Sidney might do?

Suddenly, Sidney grabbed Harry's brownie.

"Hey!" Harry snarled.

"If I can't have it, you can't either!" Sidney said, hurling the brownie in the air. Song Lee and I watched it fly up and over the playscape. It looked like a silver shooting star.

Plunk!

It landed on the top stair of the slide.

Sidney cackled. "You can get it Monday when it's nice and **stale**!" Then he ran over to play with the other kids on the grass.

Why can't Harry get the brownie?

Harry gritted his teeth, clinched his fist, and mumbled two words, "Brownie revenge!"

"Time to line up!" Miss Mackle said.

Everyone lined up.

When we got to the school door, Harry said, "Uh-oh, I forgot my jacket!"

Miss Mackle thought about it for a minute. "Song Lee, would you go with him, please."

"Yes, Miss Mackle," Song Lee said.

The teacher fanned herself. "We'll be inside the building waiting for you where it's air-conditioned."

> What do you think Harry is planning to do?

I stood by the glass door while Sidney and everybody else lined up for drinks.

I watched Harry and Song Lee take off like horses in the Kentucky Derby. As soon as they got to the playground, Harry grabbed his jacket, then ducked under the yellow ribbon. Quickly, he tiptoed over the rubber mat, and hustled up the stairs to the slide. When he got to the top step, he held up his brownie like it was a silver trophy.

Then Harry motioned for Song Lee to come up.

Song Lee shook her head.

Harry motioned again.

Song Lee shook her head a second time. She always follows the rules.

When Harry motioned a third time, Song Lee looked both ways. No one was on the playground.

Quickly, she ducked under the yellow ribbon, tiptoed over the rubber mat, and scooted up the stairs! I couldn't believe it! When she got to the top, she sat down beside Harry on the slide.

WHOOOOOSH!

Down they went.

When they took their first spiral turn, Song Lee's hair tickled Harry's face.

Whooooooossh! They took the second spiral. Just before they got to the bottom, they swept through the dark tunnel.

Wheeeeeeee!

When they landed on the soft rubber mat, they put their hands in the air.

Then the two of them raced back to the building. I never said a thing. Their secret ride was safe with me.

> What secret did Harry and Song Lee have?

That afternoon, Harry carried out his brownie revenge on our way home from school. As soon as Harry spotted Sidney, he started waving his brownie in the air.

"Hey!" Sidney gasped. "You got your brownie back! You went on the slide!"

"Yup," Harry admitted.

"I'm telling on you!"

"Yeah? What if I give you the brownie?"

Suddenly, Sidney changed his mind. "Well...I wouldn't tell then."

"It's yours!" Harry said tossing it to him.

Sidney caught the brownie with both hands, unwrapped the foil and took a bite. "Mmmmm... it's chocolaty."

"I'm a good cook," Harry bragged.

Sidney popped the rest of the brownie in his mouth. "Mmmmm. Nice and crunchy," he said licking his fingers.

"The crunchy part is my secret ingredient."

"What's the crunchy part, Harry?" Sidney asked.

"Cockroaches."

"Aauuuuuuuugh! You tricked me!" Sidney howled as he held his throat.

Then he ran home for water.

> Do you really think that Harry put cockroaches in his brownies?

I looked at Harry.

"Did you really put cockroaches in your brownies?"

"Nah. The crunchy part is just almonds."

"Phew!" I sighed.

"Actually," Harry added, "Sidney got an A+ brownie. It was my thank-you for that sweet ride on the slide with Song Lee. After all, if it weren't for Sidney, it never would have happened!"

I laughed. Even when Harry says thank you, it can be horrible!

Talking About the Story

- Ask students to describe how Harry's brownies caused all sorts of problems, but also produced some good results.
- Ask students if they have ever cooked or baked a special treat for family or friends. Have them describe what they have made or would like to make.

Vocabulary in Action

spiral

In the story the slide on the new playscape is shaped like a spiral. Something that is spiral winds around and around, with each curve either above or outside the one before it.

- Ask students which is a spiral, a path in the park or a winding staircase. Why?
- Ask a volunteer to draw something spiral-shaped on the board.

abrupt

Harry abruptly announces that he has made brownies. If something is abrupt, it is very quick and sometimes unpleasant.

- Ask students which action is abrupt, practicing for next week's baseball game or canceling today's game because of rain. Why do you say that?
- Have students pantomime an abrupt change in their mood, from happy to sad.

ceremony

The kids at school were supposed to wait for a special ceremony before they could play on the playscape. A ceremony is an event during which special things are done or said.

- Ask students which is most likely to be a ceremony, a wedding or lunch at school. Why?
- Have students describe ceremonies they have attended.

stale

Sidney teases Harry by saying that the brownie will be stale before he gets to eat it. When something is stale, it is no longer fresh.

- Ask students which is stale, a ripe peach or a piece of dry bread. Why?
- Ask students to describe the taste of stale foods, such as brownies, cookies, chips, crackers, etc.

Words About the Story

persuade

Sidney keeps begging Harry to give him a brownie. In other words, Sidney was trying to persuade Harry. When you persuade someone, you get them to think it's a good idea to do something.

- Ask students if they would persuade a child to play outside during a storm or to wear a helmet when riding a bike. Why?
- Have pairs of students take turns trying to persuade each other to do a chore, such as take out the trash or walk a dog.

disgust

Harry does some things that others dislike. His behavior sometimes disgusts other people. Disgust is a strong feeling of dislike for something.

- Ask which would be more disgusting, a classmate telling you to eat a worm or a friend inviting you to play.
- Ask students to make a face as if they were looking at something disgusting.

deceive

Harry said there were cockroaches in his brownies, but it wasn't true. Harry deceived Sidney. If you deceive someone, you make them believe something that is not true.

- Ask students which is deceiving someone, borrowing a book or keeping a CD that you promised to return. Why?
- Ask how an animal's appearance might be deceiving.

The Astronaut and the Onion

In this story Gloria's trip to the store for an onion turns into an encounter with a person who is "out of this world."

Vocabulary

Words From the Story

These words appear in blue in the story. You might wish to go over their meanings briefly before reading the story.

display
To display something is to show it to others.

paralyzed
If you are paralyzed, you can't move your body.

warp
A warp is something that is twisted or bent.

tilt
If you tilt something, you move it so that one end is higher than the other.

orbit
When you orbit something, you move around it.

Words About the Story

These words will be introduced after the story is read, using context from the story.

achieve   **coincidence**

Getting Ready for the Read-Aloud

Show students the picture on page 78 of Gloria and a woman standing in a checkout line at the supermarket. Read aloud the title. Explain that when Gloria has a chance meeting with a famous astronaut in a grocery store, she discovers something important about herself.

Encourage students to share what they know about astronauts and the jobs they do. Do they think they have what it takes to become an astronaut? Why or why not?

The following words occur in the story. They can be briefly explained as you come to them in the story: *continents*, large masses of land that are divided into countries; *universe*, everything that exists, including Earth, the other planets, and the stars.

The Astronaut and the Onion

By Ann Cameron

Illustrated by Andrea Kantrowitz

My mother was making spaghetti sauce. She said, "Gloria, honey, would you go buy me an onion?"

"Sure," I said. She gave me some money, and I went.

The store was crowded with old people holding tightly to their shopping carts, little kids hollering to their parents for candy, and lots of people staring at shopping lists and blocking the aisles.

I ducked around all the carts and went to the back where the vegetables are. From all the onions in the bin, I took the prettiest—a big round one, light tan and shiny, with a silvery glow to its skin.

I carried it to the express checkout and stood at the end of a very long line.

Next to me there was a giant Berkbee's Baby Food **display**. It was like a wall of glass, and taller than I am. All the little jars were stacked up to look like a castle, with pennants that said "Baby Power" sticking out above the castle doorways and windows. At the top there was a high tower with a red-and-white flag that said "Berkbee's Builds Better Babies!" I started counting the jars, but when I got to 346, I gave up. There must have been at least a thousand.

The checkout line didn't move. To pass the time, I started tossing my onion from hand to hand. I tried to improve and make my throws harder to catch.

A woman wearing a sky-blue jogging suit got in line behind me. She was holding a cereal box. She smiled at me, and I smiled back.

I decided to show her what a really good catcher I am. I made a wild and daring onion throw.

I missed the catch. The onion kept going, straight for the middle of the baby food castle. The castle was going to fall!

Bringing the Story to Life

The story gives a vivid description of Gloria's nearly disastrous onion toss. The toss, and Gloria's response when it goes wrong, can be dramatized with simple arm motions and facial expressions.

My folks would have to pay for every broken jar! The store manager would kill me. After that, my folks would bring me back to life to tell me things that would be much worse than death.

I was **paralyzed**. I shut my eyes.

I didn't hear a crash. Maybe I had gone deaf from fright. Or maybe I was in a time **warp** because of my fear. In fifty years the onion would land, and that would be the end of me.

I felt a tap on my shoulder. If I opened my eyes, I would see the store manager and all the broken jars.

I didn't want to see him. I didn't want to know how bad it was.

Why didn't Gloria want to open her eyes?

There came a tap again, right on the top of my head.

I heard a woman's voice. "I have your onion."

I opened my eyes. The woman in the jogging suit handed the onion to me.

"Lucky I used to play baseball," she said.

"O-o-o-h," I said. I clutched the onion.

"O-o-o-h," I moaned again.

"You're welcome," was all she said.

She had brown eyes with a sparkle in them, and her hair was in shiny black ringlets. She wore blue-green earrings that hung on tiny gold chains. When she **tilted** her head, her earrings spun around, and I saw they were the Earth—I mean, made to look like the Earth, jeweled with green continents and blue oceans.

"Your earrings are beautiful," I said

She smiled. "Some friends got them for me," she said, "to remind me of a trip we made."

When she said "trip," her face started to look familiar, but I didn't know why. Then I remembered.

Who do you think this person might be? What clues do you have?

"I've seen you!" I said. "I saw you on TV!"

She smiled. "Could be."

"And you come from right here in town, but you don't live here anymore," I said.

"That's right," she said.

"And you are—aren't you?—Dr. Grace Street, the astronaut!"

She tilted her head, and the little Earths on both her ears spun around. "That's me," she said.

I was amazed, because I never thought I would meet a famous person in my life, and yet one was right beside me in the supermarket, and I myself, Gloria Jones, was talking to her, all because of my onion throw.

"We learned about the space station in school last year," I said. "You were up there, **orbiting** the Earth."

"My team and I were there," Dr. Street said.

"What is space like?"

"You know," she said.

"How could I know?" I said.

"We're always in space," Dr. Street said. "We're in space right now."

"Yes," I said, "but what was it like out there, where you went? Out there it must seem different."

"Do you really want to know?" she asked, and I said yes.

"The most awesome part was when we had to fix things on the outside of the station. We got our jobs done and floated in our space suits, staring out into the universe. There were zillions of stars—and space, deep and black, but it didn't seem exactly empty. It seemed to be calling to us, calling us to go on an endless journey. And that was very scary.

> Why did space seem scary to Dr. Street?

"So we turned and looked at Earth. We were two hundred miles above it. We saw enormous swirls of clouds and the glow of snowfields at the poles. We saw water like a giant blue cradle for the land. One big ocean, not 'oceans.' The Earth isn't really chopped up into countries, either. Up there you see it is one great big powerful living being that knows a lot, a lot more than we do."

"What does it know?" I said.

"It knows how to be Earth," Dr. Street said. "And that's a lot."

I tried to imagine everything she had seen. It gave me a shiver.

"I wish I could see what you saw," I said. "I'd like to be an astronaut. Of course, probably I couldn't."

Dr. Street frowned. "Why do you say 'Probably I couldn't?'"

"Practically nobody gets to do that," I said.

"You might be one of the people who do," she said. "But you'll never do anything you want to do if you keep saying 'Probably I couldn't.'"

"But maybe I can't!" I protested. I looked down at my onion. I didn't think a very poor onion thrower had a chance to be an astronaut.

Dr. Street looked at my onion, too. "It was a good throw—just a bad catch," she said. "Anyhow—saying 'Maybe I can't' is different. It's okay. It's realistic.

"Even 'I can't' can be a good, sensible thing to say. It makes life simpler. When you really know you can't do one thing, that leaves you time to try some of the rest. But when you don't even know what you can do, telling yourself 'Probably I couldn't' will stop you before you even start. It's paralyzing. You don't want to be paralyzed, do you?"

"I was just paralyzed," I said. "A minute ago, when I threw my onion. I didn't enjoy it one bit."

"If you don't want to be paralyzed," Dr. Street said, "be careful what you tell yourself—because whatever you tell yourself you're very likely to believe."

I thought about what she said. "If maybe I could be an astronaut," I asked, "how would I get to be one?"

Why did Gloria think that she could never be an astronaut?

"You need to do well in school," she said. "And you need to tame your fears. Not get rid of them—just tame them."

The line moved forward suddenly, and we moved up. Maybe the people in line behind us thought Dr. Street and I were mother and daughter having a serious conversation, because they left some space around us.

"So how does a person tame fears?"

"By doing things that are difficult and succeeding," Dr. Street said. "That's how you learn you can count on yourself. That's how you get confidence. But even then, you keep a little bit of fear inside—a fear that keeps you careful."

The checkout line moved again and we moved with it.

"Big things are really little," Dr. Street said. "That's a great secret of life."

"How—" I began. But I never got to ask how big things are really little, because I was the first person in line.

The checkout man looked at my onion.

"Young lady, didn't you weigh that?" he asked.

"No, sir," I said.

"Go back to Produce and have it weighed."

So I had to go.

"Goodbye," Dr. Street said.

"Goodbye," I said. On the way to Produce, I looked back at her. She was walking toward the exit with her cereal box. I waved, but she didn't notice.

And I could see how little things are really big. Just on account of an onion, I had met an astronaut, and on account of that same onion, I had to stop talking to her.

But how big things are really little I couldn't understand at all.

Talking About the Story

- Ask students to describe how Gloria's ordinary trip to the store ended with a very special surprise.
- Ask students if they have ever had an unexpected meeting that ended up being very meaningful. Have them describe the meeting.

Vocabulary in Action

paralyzed

Gloria was paralyzed when she thought the onion would knock down the display. If you are paralyzed, you can't move your body.

- Ask students which event might paralyze someone, seeing a large spider or watching a funny movie. Explain your answer.
- Ask students to describe a time when they've felt paralyzed by fear.

tilt

Dr. Street tilts her head, and her Earth earrings spin. If you tilt something, you move it so that one end is higher than the other.

- Ask students which thing might be more easily tilted, a picture hanging on a wall or a windowsill. Explain why.
- Ask students to hold up a book or notebook and tilt it with one end higher than the other.

display

Gloria tosses an onion that nearly hits a display of baby food. To display something is to show it to others.

- Ask students where they would most likely see a display of vegetables, in a garden or at a grocery store. Why do you think so?
- Have a pair of students set up a display of objects in the class.

warp

Gloria talks about feeling like she is in a time warp, where time seems to go on and on. A warp is something that is twisted or bent.

- Ask students which seems like a time warp, waiting in a long line or riding a bike. Why?
- Have students take turns showing how they would move in a time warp.

orbit

Gloria asks Dr. Street about orbiting Earth in a space shuttle. When you orbit something, you move around it.

- Ask students which thing might orbit Earth, a satellite or a bird. Why?
- Call on several students to walk in an orbit around another student.

Words About the Story

achieve

Dr. Street encourages Gloria to achieve her goals. When you achieve something, you have done well and completed something very hard.

- Ask students which would be a big achievement, climbing a mountain or riding in a car on a mountain road. Explain why.
- Have students describe achievements that they are particularly proud of.

coincidence

Gloria's meeting with Dr. Street is a coincidence. A coincidence is when two things just happen but seem like they go together.

- Ask students which situation would be a coincidence, meeting three friends by chance at the store or planning to play with your best friend after school. Why do you think so?
- Ask pairs of students to act out a scene where there is a coincidence.

Returning the Enemy's Dog

This true story tells about an act of kindness performed by our country's first President, George Washington.

Vocabulary

Words From the Story

These words appear in blue in the story. You might wish to go over their meanings briefly before reading the story.

confirm
If you confirm something, you show that it is true.

indicate
When you indicate something to someone else, you show them where it is or that it exists.

gracious
If someone is gracious, they are polite and thoughtful.

inscription
An inscription is writing that is carved into something, like metal, stone, or wood.

Words About the Story

These words will be introduced after the story is read, using context from the story.

humane   **diplomat**   **integrity**

Getting Ready for the Read-Aloud

Show students the picture on page 86 and explain that this painting shows George Washington, who became the first President of the United States.

In this story, George Washington is not President yet; he is a general fighting a war. Ask students to describe what they think a general does in his job. Read the title of the story. Ask students how the title might be related to Washington's duties as a general.

The following words occur in the story. They can be briefly explained as you come to them in the story: *legend*, a made-up story about a real person; *character*, someone's good and bad qualities.

Returning the Enemy's Dog

By Rochelle Rupp

Bringing the Story to Life

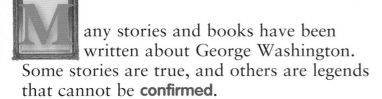any stories and books have been written about George Washington. Some stories are true, and others are legends that cannot be **confirmed**.

For instance, it is true that Washington had false teeth, but they were not wooden. He wore cow's teeth, hippo's teeth, and teeth made of elephant ivory and walrus ivory. He even wore other people's teeth—but he did not wear wooden teeth.

We have no records that **indicate** that young George actually chopped down his father's prized cherry tree and then later admitted bravely, "I cannot tell a lie." We do know that he was a brave soldier, a **gracious** man, and a wise president.

This story gives an account of a historical event. In order to set the scene, you may want to display several illustrations of George Washington from textbooks or other classroom materials.

> What are some things we know about George Washington?

One true story that demonstrates Washington's good character comes from a letter written during the Revolutionary War when America was not yet its own country. At that time it was an English colony, which means it belonged to England. Many American colonists wanted to be free from England, so America declared its independence from England and then went to war. The war was called the American Revolution, and George Washington commanded the Continental Army during the Revolutionary War.

Many American soldiers, including General Washington, brought their dogs to war. Dogs helped hunt for food, guarded against wild animals, and kept the soldiers from feeling lonely while they were away from their homes and families.

> Why did soldiers bring their dogs to war? Do you think this was a good idea?

The King of England wanted America to remain an English colony, so he sent soldiers to America to fight in the war. The general of the King's Army was named

William Howe. He sailed to America with over 9,000 soldiers. Like George Washington, General Howe brought his dog to war, too.

In the fall of 1777, Washington's troops went to Pennsylvania to fight against General Howe's troops. It was a dreadful battle, and when the fighting ended for the day George noticed a dog wandering alone on the battlefield. The dog looked lost, but he was wearing a collar. The soldiers bent down to read the name on the dog's collar. The owner of the dog was William Howe! He was the general of the enemy army!

> What do you think George Washington will do with this dog?

Washington believed that the dog should be returned to his master, even though the master was the general of the enemy's army. George asked Alexander Hamilton to write a letter to General Howe. The letter politely explained that the American army had found General Howe's dog and that General Washington wanted to return the dog to his master.

The letter said:

General Washington's compliments to General Howe, [he] does himself the pleasure to return him a Dog, which accidentally fell into his hands, and by the **inscription** *on the Collar, appears to belong to General Howe.*

October 6th, 1777.

The Revolutionary War continued on for six more years, and in 1783 America won independence and became its very own country. After the war, George Washington became the first President of the United States. His dogs joined him then, too.

Talking About the Story

- Ask students to describe how George Washington encountered his enemy's dog, and what he decided to do with it.
- Ask students if they have ever done something nice for someone. How did it feel to be able to do this?

Vocabulary in Action

Words From the Story

confirm

Legends are stories that cannot be confirmed. If you confirm something, you show that it is true.

- Ask students which is the best way to confirm the spelling of a word, by asking a friend or by checking a dictionary. Explain why.
- Call on a volunteer to confirm the number of students in the class by counting.

indicate

Records indicate that some stories about George Washington are true. When you indicate something to someone else, you show them where it is or that it exists.

- Ask which would indicate that you are happy, a smile or a groan. Why do you say so?
- Ask students to indicate where in the school they would find safety features such as exits, fire alarms, and fire extinguishers.

gracious

George Washington's actions in the story are gracious. If someone is gracious, they are polite and thoughtful.

- Ask students if you might be gracious when you're having a party or when you're doing the laundry. Why?
- Ask pairs of students to act out something a gracious person might do.

inscription

The inscription on the collar of the lost dog showed that the dog belonged to General Howe. An inscription is writing that is carved into something, like metal, stone, or wood.

- Ask which thing would most likely have an inscription, a stuffed animal or the base of a statue. Explain your answer.
- Ask students to write an inscription that might appear on a statue.

Words About the Story

humane

George Washington returned General Howe's dog. He was humane. If someone is humane, they act in a kind way to other people and animals.

- Ask which is humane, putting out a bird feeder or letting your dog run free in the street. Why?
- Call on students to describe how to treat a pet humanely.

diplomat

George Washington sent a letter to General Howe and returned his dog. He acted as a diplomat. A diplomat is a person who works for their country by talking to other countries about problems they need to solve together.

- Ask students when you might act as a diplomat, during a quarrel or during silent reading. Why?
- Ask one student to act as a diplomat to help groups with differing viewpoints come to an agreement.

integrity

George Washington's actions were fair. He had integrity. If you have integrity, you are honest and true to your beliefs.

- Ask which situation best shows integrity, admitting a mistake or blaming someone else. Explain your answer.
- Ask students to describe a time when someone they know acted with integrity.

Harriet Hare Tells All

In this story Harriet Hare tells the "true" story of the Tortoise and the Hare.

Vocabulary

Words From the Story

These words appear in blue in the story. You might wish to go over their meanings briefly before reading the story.

ordinary

If something is ordinary, it is common and not special in any way.

scowl

When you scowl, you frown as if you are very angry.

mischievous

A mischievous person likes to play tricks on other people.

scan

When you scan something, you look at it quickly to find important or interesting information.

Words About the Story

These words will be introduced after the story is read, using context from the story.

apology   **ambitious**   **sympathy**

Getting Ready for the Read-Aloud

Show students the picture on page 91 of the hare and the tortoise. Read the title aloud and tell students that a hare is like a rabbit and the turtle-like animal is a tortoise. Ask what the hare might want to tell about.

Recall the story about the tortoise and the hare who had a race. Point out that tortoises are usually very slow and hares very fast. Explain that in the story the tortoise wins the race because he kept going when the hare stopped to take a nap.

The following words occur in the story. They can be briefly explained as you come to them in the story: *demonstrate*, to show how to do something; *stopwatch*, a kind of watch that can be stopped to tell the exact amount of time something takes; *trudging*, walking as if it is hard to do.

Harriet Hare Tells All

By Lewis Hoff
Illustrated by David Hohn

*H*i, I'm Harriet Hare. You know, I made a mistake by letting every animal in the forest think my neighbor Torry Tortoise beat me in a race last year. Even Torry himself believes he beat me, too. Why, just the other day, I was telling him how he could run faster if he just picked up his knees. You know what he said? "I don't have to do things fast to be good, Harriet. Of all the animals in this forest, you should know THAT!" And then he laughed at me!

Vary your reading tempo to represent the two main characters. Read Harriet Hare's words as quickly as possible without jeopardizing comprehension, and read Torry Tortoise's words very slowly.

But the truth of the story is that there never was a race between *this* hare and *that* tortoise. Nope. Never was. That's why I'm here tell you what *really* happened.

It was an **ordinary** day in the forest. I was jogging down the path like I always do, waving to the animals as I passed. But I was very surprised to see Torry. He was dressed in shorts and a T-shirt and looked like he was going to exercise.

"Hi, Torry!" I called out cheerfully. "Are you going to jog?"

"Yes," answered Torry. "I'm not as snappy as I used to be, though. I need to get in better shape, but I'm not sure how to start."

Well, I felt very sorry for Torry. After all, how would you like to carry your home around all the time? I decided that I would be a good neighbor and offer my expert advice to Torry.

What problem did Torry have? How could Harriet help him?

"I know a lot about running," I said. "I would be happy to help you."

Torry suddenly began to **scowl** at me. "No, thank you," he answered grumpily. "You would play a trick on me like you always do."

Sadly, Torry was right. I am very **mischievous** at times, especially when it comes to Torry. Tortoises just take so long to do anything!

How will Harriet show Torry that she's sorry about how she's treated him in the past?

"I do admit that I have played many tricks on you," I said. "But I am very sorry. Hey…what if I make it up to you by being your personal trainer? With my help, you will be a terrific, trim Torry Tortoise in no time. I'll even bet that we can get you running faster in just a week or two."

Torry agreed, but he was still a little worried. "A week or two!" gasped Torry. "That seems really hard. Do you honestly think I can do it?"

"With my help, you can do anything!" I answered.

We began to warm up with some knee bends. I did a few to demonstrate, and then it was Torry's turn. When Torry bent his knees, however, they disappeared right into his shell along with his head and arms. When he stood up again, his head and arms popped out. He looked just like a turtle-in-the-box toy! I had to get Torry to stop before I laughed out loud. I certainly didn't want to hurt his feelings again.

What happened when Torry tried to do knee bends?

"That's enough stretching," I said. "Let's see how far and how fast you can run. I'll jog ahead of you and stop at different places along the path. When you run past, I'll time you with my stopwatch."

We agreed that the first stop would be by the river. I would run ahead and wait there for Torry.

"Ready, set, go!" I yelled. I started the stopwatch and raced off. I noticed Mrs. Cardinal fly into a tree and waved as I sprinted ahead of Torry. For some reason, she gave me a funny look. However, I didn't have time to talk.

Why did Mrs. Cardinal give Harriet a funny look?

I got to the river in three minutes, and sat down to wait for Torry. Soon, I saw him trudging slowly along the path.

"You're racing right along, Torry!" I called. "You got here in seven minutes. Why don't you run to that big rock farther down the path?"

Torry let out a deep breath and waved. "I can do this!" he puffed.

I got up and sped past Torry. By now, I noticed several animals peeking out from behind the trees. I waved to them, but they just frowned at me. There must be a problem. I would have to find out what it was later, though.

Why were the animals frowning?

I ran to the rock as fast as I could. I was out of breath myself and looked at the stopwatch. I had run the distance in less than four minutes. That was the best time I had ever run that distance! I sat down to catch my breath.

After awhile I began to **scan** the forest path. Torry was slowly plodding along. I yelled, "Congratulations, Torry! You just ran another eight minutes. I know you can finish the whole trail. Think of this jog as a race!"

Unfortunately, as I raised my arms to cheer, the stopwatch flew out of my hands and into the bushes. Just then, Torry jogged right past me. I had to find the watch before I could catch up to Torry! It took several minutes, but I found it. Then I was off. I ran after Torry like… well, like a rabbit.

As I got near the end of the path, I saw all the forest animals waiting there. They were yelling and cheering for Torry! This support was just what Torry needed to encourage him to finish. But Torry was going to reach the end before I could get there to time him. I had to run even faster, but many of the animals were blocking the path as they cheered for Torry.

What do the animals think is happening? What do you think will happen next? Why do you think that?

"Let me through!" I yelled. "I have to finish before Torry!"

"Shame on you, Harriet," said Mrs. Cardinal. "How could you think about racing that little tortoise?"

"And everyone thinks I'm sly and mean," added Mr. Fox. "At least I've never picked on a turtle!"

I couldn't believe what everyone was saying. They thought I was racing Torry! How did this happen?

Just as I got through the crowd, I saw them lift Torry high over their heads like he was a hero. Torry looked so happy. I just didn't have the heart to say anything. So now everyone believes that Torry and I had a race and that the slow and steady tortoise won! But now you know the truth.

You believe me, don't you?

Talking About the Story

- Ask students to compare Harriet Hare's version of the story to the more familiar version. Then have a student explain why Harriet's version differs.

- Ask students if they ever found out that their understanding of an event was completely different from the way someone else understood the same event. Have them share what happened.

Vocabulary in Action

ordinary

Harriet says that her story began on an ordinary day in the forest. If something is ordinary, it is common and not special in any way.

- Ask students which is an ordinary breakfast, a bowl of cereal or waffles with strawberries and whipped cream. Why do you think so?
- Have a student draw a picture of an ordinary house.

mischievous

Harriet admits that she is sometimes mischievous. A mischievous person likes to play tricks on other people.

- Ask who is more likely to be mischievous, a clown or a doctor. Why is that?
- Have a group of students pretend to do something mischievous.

apology

Harriet offers an apology to Torry. An apology is something you say or write to show someone that you are sorry for what you have done.

- Ask which someone might apologize for, breaking a chair or breaking a record. Explain why.
- Call on a student to act as if he or she were offering an apology for something that he or she did.

scowl

Torry scowls at Harriet when she offers to help him. When you scowl, you frown as if you are very angry.

- Ask students which might cause someone to scowl, being told they have no homework or being told they have to redo their homework. Why?
- Call on a student to make a face as if he or she were scowling at something.

scan

In the story Harriet scans the forest path, looking for Torry. When you scan something, you look at it quickly to find important or interesting information.

- Ask which you might scan before a test, a textbook or a calendar. Why?
- Ask students to act as if they are scanning the classroom for a lost book.

ambitious

Torry is ambitious. An ambitious person wants to do well in their work.

- Ask who is more ambitious, a girl who does extra work or a girl who barely finishes her homework. Why?
- Ask students to act as if they were ambitious and talk about some of the things that they plan to accomplish.

sympathy

Harriet has sympathy for Torry. If you have sympathy for someone, you show them that you share their sadness for whatever troubles they have.

- Ask which you might have sympathy for, a pampered poodle or a frightened mutt. Why do you say that?
- Ask two students to act out how they would show sympathy for a friend who has sprained an ankle.

Nine GOLD Medals

In this poem nine athletes show that they are winners by working as a team to finish a race in the Special Olympics.

Vocabulary

Words From the Poem

These words appear in blue in the poem. You might wish to go over their meanings briefly before reading the poem.

spectators

Spectators are those who watch a sports contest or other public happening.

poised

If someone is poised to do something, they are ready to spring into action at any moment.

anguish

When you feel so bad in your body or in your mind that you can hardly stand it, you feel anguish.

ovation

When an audience claps long and hard for someone, they are giving that person an ovation.

beaming

When your face shows great joy, you are beaming.

Words About the Poem

These words will be introduced after the poem is read, using context from the poem.

assist   **priority**

Getting Ready for the Read-Aloud

Show students the picture on page 99 of the boy and his gold medal. Read the title aloud and explain that a gold medal is awarded to the person who finishes in first place in a race or a contest.

Explain that the poem takes place at an event called the Special Olympics. Ask students to share what they might already know about the Special Olympics. If necessary, explain that this event is an athletic competition in a variety of Olympic-type sports for students and adults with developmental challenges.

The following words occur in the poem. They can be briefly explained as you come to them in the poem: *athletes*, people who are very good at sports or games; *resolved*, deciding that you will try hard to do something; *asphalt*, a black substance used to make walkways and roads; *compete*, to try hard to outdo others in a race or contest.

Nine GOLD Medals

By David Roth

Illustrated by Nicole Tadgell

Read the first three stanzas with a pace and tone that express the anticipation of the spectators and athletes waiting for the race to begin. Then punctuate the start of the race with the sound effect of the starter pistol.

The athletes had come from all over
   the country
To run for the gold, for the silver and bronze
Many weeks and months of training
All coming down to these games

The **spectators** gathered around the old field
For cheering on all the young women and men
The final event of the day was approaching
Excitement grew high to begin

The blocks were all lined up for those who would
   use them
The hundred-yard dash was the race to be run
There were nine resolved athletes in back of the
   starting line
Poised for the sound of the gun

> What was about to happen?

The signal was given, the pistol exploded
And so did the runners all charging ahead
But the smallest among them, he stumbled
   and staggered
And fell to the asphalt instead

He gave out a cry in frustration and **anguish**
His dreams and his efforts all dashed in the dirt
But as sure as I'm standing here telling this story
The same goes for what next occurred

> What happened to the smallest runner?

The eight other runners pulled up on their heels
The ones who had trained for so long to compete
One by one they all turned around and went back
   to help him
And brought the young boy to his feet

How did the eight
other runners help the
smallest runner?

Then all the nine runners joined hands and continued
The hundred-yard dash now reduced to a walk
And a banner above that said "Special Olympics"
Could not have been more the mark

That's how the race ended, with nine gold medals
They came to the finish line holding hands still
And a standing **ovation** and nine **beaming** faces
Said more than these words ever will

Talking About the Poem

- Have students summarize the race in their own words and tell how this race was different from other races they may have watched or taken part in.
- Ask students to describe why "Nine Gold Medals" was a good title for this poem.

Vocabulary in Action

spectators

In the story spectators gathered around the field to cheer on the athletes. Spectators are those who watch a sports contest or other public happening.

- Ask students where they might see spectators, at a doctor's office or at a football game. Why?
- Have students describe what is appropriate behavior for spectators at various events.

poised

Nine athletes were poised for the sound of the gun that would begin the race. If someone is poised to do something, they are ready to spring into action at any moment.

- Ask when a horse would be poised, while running around the track or at the starting line. Explain.
- Have students pantomime how they would look poised at a starting line.

anguish

The smallest runner gave out a cry in anguish. When you feel so bad in your body or your mind that you can hardly stand it, you feel anguish.

- Ask students which might cause someone to feel anguish, climbing a tree or falling off a branch. Why?
- Have students use their voice and body to show how someone in anguish might feel.

ovation

The spectators gave the nine athletes a standing ovation. When an audience claps long and hard for someone, they are giving that person an ovation.

- Ask which audience is giving an ovation, the one that is watching a play or the one that is clapping. Why?
- Have small groups of students give a standing ovation for the rest of the group.

beaming

All nine athletes had beaming faces at the end of the race. When your face shows great joy, you are beaming.

- Ask when someone might be beaming, when they are squinting their eyes in the bright sunlight or when they are posing for a picture after winning a medal. Explain.
- Have students show how they might beam with joy.

Words About the Poem

assist

The eight other runners went back to help the smallest runner. Another way to say this is to say that they assisted the smallest runner. To assist is to help.

- Ask students when they might want to assist, when a friend doesn't know how to read a certain word or when a friend is taking a test in class. Why?
- Have one student pretend to sprain an ankle and another show how someone might assist him or her.

priority

Helping the smallest runner was a priority to the other runners. When something is a priority, it is so important that you do it before anything else.

- Ask students which would be a priority if the fire alarm in school sounded, to form a line and quietly leave the building or clean their desks. Why?
- Ask students to prioritize the day's activities. What are the most important things they have to do? The least?

The LIZARD and the SUN

In this Mexican folk tale a brave little lizard won't give up until she brings light and warmth back to the world.

Vocabulary

Words From the Story

These words appear in blue in the story. You might wish to go over their meanings briefly before reading the story.

majestic
Something that is majestic seems great and powerful.

vendor
A vendor is a person who sells something.

adorn
When you adorn something, you put things on it to make it look more beautiful.

emerald
Something that is emerald is deep green in color.

organize
When you organize something, you put it in a clear order.

Words About the Story

These words will be introduced after the story is read, using context from the story.

conceal   **restore**

Getting Ready for the Read-Aloud

Show students the picture on page 104 of the lizard and the sun. Read the title aloud and have students describe the features of the desert setting.

Point out that this story is a folk tale from Mexico. Explain that a folk tale is a story that is passed down from generation to generation. Often these tales attempted to help people understand some event that occurred in nature. You may want to help students locate Mexico on a map or globe.

The LIZARD and the SUN

By Alma Flor Ada

Illustrated by Felipe Dávalos

Bringing the Story to Life

Call attention to the animals' growing frustration by emphasizing the phrase "But the sun was not there." Then read the sun's dialogue with a sleepy tone and augment it by giving an "enormous yawn" as described in the text.

T he whole world knows that the sun comes out every day. Some days, it shines brightly in a clear blue sky. Other days, clouds cover the sun and its light is much paler. When the clouds let loose their load of rain, the sun disappears behind a curtain of water. There are places where it snows. During a snowstorm, the sun also stays hidden. But even when clouds, rain, or snow hide the sun, we know that it's still there. The story I am going to tell you happened a long long time ago, when the sun had really disappeared.

It had been many days since the sun had come out. Everything was dark. All of the plants, the animals, and the people were waiting anxiously for the sun to appear. But the sun did not come out, and everything remained in darkness.

The people were cold. The birds had stopped singing, and the children had stopped playing. Everyone was worried and afraid, for this had never happened before.

Why was everyone worried and afraid?

The animals decided to go out in search of the sun. The fish and the turtles looked in the rivers and lakes. But the sun was not there.

The green frogs and the wide-mouthed toads looked through all the puddles. But the sun was not there.

The deer and the squirrels searched through the forests. But the sun was not there.

The rabbits and the hares searched through the fields. The jaguar searched through the green jungle, where he lives. But the sun was nowhere to be found.

The birds searched through the branches where they had made their nests. And the **majestic** eagle flew over the mountaintops and the cones of the volcanoes. But no one could find the sun. And little by little, all of the animals stopped looking. All of them except for the lizard.

105

The lizard kept on looking for the sun. She climbed rocks, scurried up tree trunks, and peered under leaves, searching, always searching.

Finally, one day, she saw something very strange. She was scampering over some rocks when she saw that one of them was shining as though it had a light inside.

The lizard had seen many rocks in her life. She had seen rocks that were smooth and polished, and rocks that were rough and sharp. She had seen shiny gray rocks and dull dark ones. But she had never seen a rock that shone as much as this one did. It shone so brightly that it seemed to glow. So with great excitement, the lizard ran off to the city to share her discovery.

> What strange thing did the lizard see? What did she do?

At last the lizard reached the city. Even though there had been no sunlight for many days, the people had kept on working. The barges floated softly on the waters of the lagoon, laden with fruits and flowers. In the enormous marketplace, the **vendors** had laid out their wares on beautiful woven blankets. The pyramids of fruits and vegetables looked like tiny copies of the great stone pyramids that loomed over the city.

But without the sun's light, no one could see the brilliant colors of the peppers and tomatoes, the beautiful deep colors of the blankets and shawls. Instead, the flickering torches that lit the marketplace cast deep shadows. And instead of the cheerful bustle of people buying and selling and having a good time, there was a low murmur of worried voices wondering how long this endless night might last.

> What did the lizard find when she reached the city? What was the mood of the people there?

The lizard did not stop to look at the barges or at the market's wares. She did not stop to look at the silent crowd that walked through the plaza. Instead, she headed straight for the grand palace and did not stop until she was in front of the throne.

"Sir, I have seen a rock which shone with a strange light," said the lizard.

"Move the rock, so you can see why it shines," ordered the emperor.

The lizard did what the emperor had commanded. She returned to where the rock lay and tried to move it. She tried to push it with her two front legs and then with her two hind legs. But the rock did not move. At last the lizard pushed the rock with her whole body. But the rock would not budge.

There was nothing left for the lizard to do but go back to the city. She crossed one of the wide bridges, passed by the marketplace, arrived at the grand palace, and went straight to see the emperor.

◆◆◆◆◆

What did the emperor order the lizard to do? What happened when the lizard followed his command?

She found him sitting on the same throne, surrounded by the smoke of the torches.

"I'm very sorry, sir," she said. "I did everything I could, but I could not move the rock."

The emperor wanted very much to see this glowing rock, so he decided to go back with the lizard. But first he called for the woodpecker.

"I want you to come with us," the emperor said to the woodpecker.

And so the three of them, the emperor, the lizard, and the woodpecker, went to see the glowing rock.

When they reached the rock, the emperor said to the woodpecker, "I want you to hit that rock hard with your beak."

The woodpecker obeyed the emperor. He gave the rock a sharp peck with his strong beak, and the rock split open. And inside the rock was the sun, all curled up and fast asleep.

What did they find inside the rock? What was the sun doing?

The emperor was very happy to see the sun again. The world had been very cold and dark without him.

"Wake him up, woodpecker," ordered the emperor.

And the woodpecker pecked several times on the rock.

Tock, tock, tock, went the woodpecker's beak as it struck the hard rock. The sun opened one eye, but he immediately closed it again and went right on sleeping.

"Wake up, Sun," said the lizard. "All of the animals have been looking for you."

But the sun did not answer. He just stretched a bit and went on sleeping.

"Wake up, Sun," said the woodpecker. "All of the birds have been waiting for you."

But the sun yawned an enormous yawn and kept on sleeping.

"Get up, Sun," said the emperor. "The entire city needs you."

But the sun just said, "Leave me in peace. I want to sleep."

The emperor knew that he had to do something. Without the sun, the plants could not grow, and his people would not have any food to eat. Without the sun, the children could not go out to play, the birds could not come out to sing, and the flowers would not bloom.

Did the darkness disappear when the sun was found inside the rock? Why or why not?

So the emperor said to the sun, "Wouldn't you like to see some beautiful dances? I will ask the finest musicians and dancers to play and dance for you. That will help you wake up."

"Well, if you want me to wake up, ask them to start playing their liveliest music, and to keep right on playing and dancing," answered the sun.

So the emperor called for the finest dancers and musicians. The dancers, all **adorned** with beautiful feathers of many colors, danced in the plaza in front of the highest pyramid. The loud, joyful music played on and on, and the sun woke up, climbed to the highest point in the sky, and shone down over everyone, lighting the whole earth.

> How did the emperor get the sun to shine again?

The emperor called for the **emerald**-colored lizard. He put her on the palm of his hand, and thanked her for having helped to find the sun. Then he called for the red-breasted woodpecker. He asked him to stand on his shoulder, and thanked him for having helped to wake up the sun.

Every year from then on, the emperor **organized** a great feast, with joyful music and beautiful dances, so that the sun would never again fall asleep, hidden away inside a rock.

And since that day, all lizards love to lie in the sun. They like to remember the day when one of their own found the sun's hiding place and helped bring him back to give light and warmth to everyone.

Talking About the Story

- Have students tell in their own words how the lizard helped bring the sun's light and warmth back to the world.
- Ask students to describe how their own lives would be different if the sun didn't come out every day.

Vocabulary in Action

majestic

In the story the majestic eagle flew over the mountaintops. Something that is majestic seems great and powerful.

- Ask students which is majestic, an ocean or a pond. Why do you think so?
- Have students pantomime how the majestic eagle may have looked as he flew.

adorn

The dancers were adorned with beautiful feathers of many colors. When you adorn something, you put things on it to make it look more beautiful.

- Ask which is adorned, a bike decorated with streamers and flags or a bike with new pedals. Explain why.
- Encourage students to help adorn the classroom by planning a display or decorating a bulletin board.

vendor

Vendors laid out their wares on beautiful woven blankets in the marketplace. A vendor is a person who sells something.

- Ask students where they might see a vendor, in their kitchen or at a baseball game. Explain your answer.
- Have volunteers role-play the actions of vendors and customers as they sell and buy things in the marketplace.

emerald

The emperor thanked the emerald-colored lizard for helping to find the sun. Something that is emerald is deep green in color.

- Ask which is emerald, a tree's leaves in the summer or sunflower petals. Why?
- Have children identify and name objects in the classroom that are emerald.

organize

The emperor organized a great feast with joyful music and beautiful dances. When you organize something, you put it in a clear order.

- Ask students which is organized, a big box of stamps or a stamp collection displayed in an album. Explain why.
- Display a group of objects and have students organize them in different ways.

conceal

The sun was concealed inside the rock. To conceal something is to hide it.

- Ask which is concealed, a snake under a pile of leaves or a snake hanging from a tree. Why do you think so?
- Have students draw a yellow sun on a sheet of paper and then show how they would conceal the sun.

restore

The lizard restored the sun. To restore something is to make it like it used to be.

- Ask which would need to be restored, a bicycle that has two flat tires or a baseball glove that has never been used. Explain your answer.
- Ask students how they might restore something in nature that was in danger of being lost forever, such as fresh water or a certain kind of plant or animal.

Charlie and Tess

In this story a sheep who thinks he's a dog uses his instincts to save the rest of his flock from certain disaster.

Vocabulary

Words From the Story

These words appear in blue in the story. You might wish to go over their meanings briefly before reading the story.

frisky
A frisky animal or person has a lot of energy and acts playful.

graze
When animals graze, they eat the plants or grass in a certain area.

soothe
When you soothe someone who is angry or upset, you calm them down.

determined
If you are determined to do something, you have decided to do it and nothing will stop you.

huddle
When people or animals huddle, they move in very close to each other with their heads together.

Words About the Story

These words will be introduced after the story is read, using context from the story.

adapt   **mature**

Getting Ready for the Read-Aloud

Ask students to look at the picture of the dog and the lamb on page 112. Read the title aloud and tell students that the lamb's name is Charlie and the name of the dog is Tess.

Point out that Tess is a sheepdog and that sheepdogs help farmers take care of their sheep. Explain that one job of sheepdogs is to help keep the sheep together in a group when the farmer wants to move them from one place to another.

Introduce some words related to sheep farming that may be unfamiliar to students: *lambing*, the time of the year when lambs are born; *bleating*, the sound lambs and sheep make; *ewe*, a female sheep; *fleece*, the wooly coat of a sheep.

Charlie and Tess

By Martin Hall
Illustrated by Catherine Walters

I t was spring, and lambing time high up in the mountains. But the weather was still cold, and snow was falling, so the farmer was out tending the flock with his sheepdog. The farmer stopped and listened. What was that noise? It sounded like a frightened bleating. Ahead he saw a tiny lamb, alone and hungry.

"My, you're a small one," the farmer said. "Can't find your mother, eh? Well, you'll just have to come home with me."

In the kitchen the farmer's daughter, Emily, made the lamb a cozy nest in a cardboard box with some old sweaters. He was very weak, but was soon sucking warm milk from a bottle.

"Let's call him Charlie," said Emily. And because they could find no ewe to take care of him, Charlie became the family's own special pet and lived with them in the farmhouse.

Bringing the Story to Life

Ask students to close their eyes and imagine that they live on a sheep farm. Paint a mental picture of a farm high in the mountains. Describe a comfortable old farmhouse and beautiful rolling hills where sheep graze.

> Why did the lamb live in the farmhouse?

The farmer's sheepdog was named Tess, and as soon as Charlie the lamb was able to skip and **frisk** around the farmyard, Tess was there to keep an eye on him. She made sure he did not stray too far and led him home at feeding time. And when Charlie was too old for the milk bottle, Tess showed him the best pastures to **graze** in.

Charlie grew quickly. Soon he was too big for the box in the kitchen, so he slept outside in Tess' doghouse. It was a tight squeeze, but Tess and Charlie didn't mind. For they were friends, and kept each other warm.

They played together when Tess was not working. The farmer would throw a ball and watch them both chase it. Of course, Tess was faster than Charlie, but often she would let the lamb win.

"Sometimes I wonder if Charlie is turning into a dog," Emily's mother said one day as the family watched him play.

In what ways was Charlie like a dog?

Charlie even had his own collar and leash. When Emily's mother went into town, Tess and Charlie would go along, too. People would laugh and point as Charlie trotted ahead, often carrying a newspaper in his mouth.

All too soon Charlie grew too big for the doghouse. It was time for him to join the rest of the flock.

Charlie missed his adopted family up on the mountainside, and Tess was lonely without her friend, and whined every night by her doghouse.

"Never mind, old girl," **soothed** the farmer. "We'll see Charlie soon enough when we move the flock to the next pasture."

But that was when the trouble started. As soon as the farmer and Tess began to herd the sheep to a new field, Charlie wanted to round up the flock, too.

"Charlie! Go back with the other sheep," laughed the farmer. But Charlie was **determined** to help Tess, and the farmer had to push him back into the flock again.

This went on all summer, because Charlie thought he was a sheepdog.

How does Charlie act when he joins the rest of the flock? Why do you think this happens?

Summer turned to autumn, and then it was nearly winter again. One day the sky was filled with clouds the color of slate. Charlie sniffed the air. It reminded him of a time long ago, when he was lost and alone. It grew colder and colder, and the wind began to blow. The sheep **huddled** together, but there was little shelter. Then it began to snow.

Charlie baaed anxiously. Snowflakes began to settle on his fleece. Where was Tess? Where was the farmer? If they didn't come soon, snow would bury the whole flock.

The snow piled up quickly, and some of the weaker sheep could barely walk through the drifts. If they didn't move into the valley quickly it would be too late.

Why is Charlie feeling anxious? What do you think he might do?

Charlie knew just what to do. He ran ahead of the flock, baaing loudly. He turned back and butted the other sheep, pulling at their wooly coats with his teeth. He raced backward and forward, until finally the flock began to move down the mountainside toward shelter.

The next day the storm died down, and a low sun shone orange across the snow-covered hills. The farmer was at last able to go out and search for his flock.

"I'm really worried—I don't know if we will be able to find them," he said to Tess, looking at the mountains. "The snow must be even deeper up there."

Tess ran ahead, and the farmer began to struggle up the mountainside. Suddenly the sheepdog bounded toward the farmer and started barking and tugging at his trousers.

"What have you found, girl?" he asked.

Tess led the farmer back into the valley along a narrow trail. At the end of the path the farmer stopped, amazed. His whole flock was safely gathered there in a sheltered hollow.

"Charlie! This must have been you," the farmer said. "You saved the whole flock from the snowstorm. You really are a sheepdog after all!"

"Woof!" Tess agreed.

"Baa," said Charlie proudly.

Talking About the Story

- Ask students to tell in their own words why Charlie was such a special sheep.
- Encourage students to tell about an animal they know who is very unusual. Ask them to explain why the animal is special.

Vocabulary in Action

Words From the Story

frisky

In the story Charlie the lamb is described as being frisky. A frisky animal or person has a lot of energy and acts playful.

- Ask which would be frisky, a snake or a puppy. Why?
- Have a few volunteers come to the front of the room and pretend to be frisky lambs.

soothe

The farmer soothed Tess when she was sad about Charlie leaving. When you soothe someone who is angry or upset, you calm them down.

- Ask who might need to be soothed, someone who ate a cookie or someone who cut her finger. Explain why.
- Ask pairs of students to make up skits in which one student pretends to be upset while the other tries to soothe them.

graze

Tess showed Charlie the best pastures to graze in. When animals graze, they eat the plants or grass in a certain area.

- Ask which animal would graze, a cow or a pet bird. Why?
- Ask students to pretend they are sheep grazing in a field.

determined

Charlie was determined to help Tess round up the flock. If you are determined to do something, you have decided to do it and nothing will stop you.

- Ask which shows that a baseball player is determined, working out once in a while or practicing every day. Why?
- Encourage students to share stories of times when they've been determined and it paid off.

huddle

The sheep huddled together to keep warm. When people or animals huddle, they move in very close to each other with their heads together.

- Ask which might be a reason for people to huddle, telling a secret or singing a song. Explain your answer.
- Have six students come to the front of the room and demonstrate how to huddle.

Words About the Story

adapt

The little lamb adapted to life in a house with a family and acted like a dog. To adapt means to change to fit a new situation or a new purpose.

- Ask who would have to adapt more, a person who moved to a new house in their neighborhood or a person who moved to a new country. Why do you think so?
- Ask students to show how they would adapt if the classroom suddenly became too cold.

mature

Charlie matured from a baby lamb into a grown-up sheep. When you mature, you grow and develop.

- Ask which behavior is mature, throwing temper tantrums or talking calmly about things that upset you. Explain your answer.
- Ask students to describe ways that they have matured since they were in kindergarten.

Planting Opportunity

This story tells how a poor, hard-working farmer outsmarts a wealthy but lazy landowner and teaches him a lesson.

Vocabulary

Words From the Story

These words appear in blue in the story. You might wish to go over their meanings briefly before reading the story.

gentle
Someone or something that is gentle does not hurt anyone or anything else.

abundant
When something is abundant, there is more than enough of it.

pesky
Something that keeps bothering you is pesky.

slumber
When you slumber, you sleep very deeply.

Words About the Story

These words will be introduced after the story is read, using context from the story.

idle   diligent   outsmart

Getting Ready for the Read-Aloud

Show students the picture on page 118 of the two farmers. Read the title aloud, and tell students that an opportunity is a good chance to do something that you want to do.

Explain that you need sunshine, rain, and rich soil to produce crops. A farmer must also work very hard planting seeds, pulling weeds, and harvesting the crops.

The following words occur in the story. They can be briefly explained as you come to them in the story: *nourished*, fed with substances needed for life and growth; *hammock*, a swinging bed made out of rope; *drowsily*, sleepily; *bumper*, unusually large; *cultivate*, to prepare land for growing crops; *shocks*, stalks of corn.

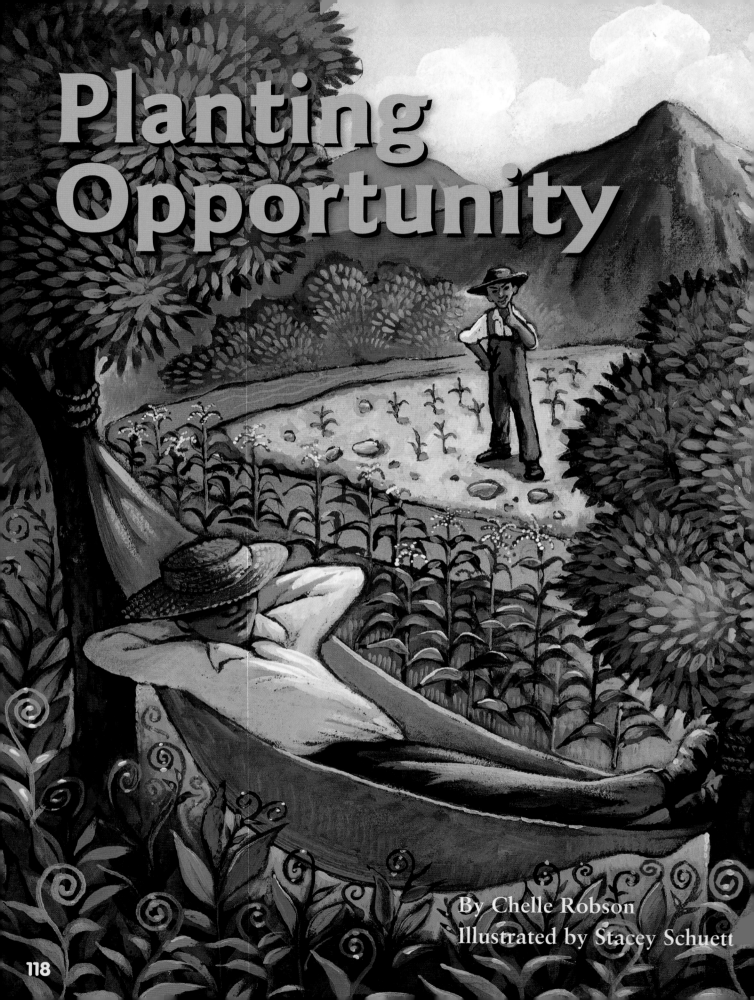

Planting Opportunity

By Chelle Robson
Illustrated by Stacey Schuett

Many years ago in a village not too far from here, there was a very wealthy man who owned all the land in the valley. His land was bursting with deep, rich soil and it was supplied by two steady streams that flowed from the nearby mountains. Warm sun and **gentle** rains nourished the fertile land, and each year the harvest was **abundant**.

As the landowner became more and more wealthy, he also became more and more lazy until finally, one winter, he decided he would no longer work the fields. He did nothing but doze all morning in the warm sun, daydream all afternoon during the gentle rains, and snore peacefully all night under the watchful moon.

On the other side of the valley, the soil was not as rich and the mountain streams were not as steady. The fields were shaded and the rains came only occasionally. After trying for many years to produce crops, a poor and hungry farmer produced an intelligent idea instead.

Bringing the Story to Life

State the farmer's words in a cheerful, confident voice and the rich landowner's words in a voice appropriate to his changing mood. Use descriptive words such as *snarled, complained,* and *drowsily*.

What happened to the landowner when he became wealthy?

He observed the lazy habits of the wealthy landowner for several seasons, and the poor farmer decided it was time to pay a visit.

"Hello, neighbor! Yes, hello. It's a fine, fine morning," the poor farmer called out.

The lazy landowner woke briefly from his nap, rolled over on his hammock, and returned to his pleasant dream.

"I have a proposition for you, neighbor. Yes, indeed, it's an offer you cannot pass up," continued the farmer. "Your good fields are going to waste and my hard efforts are fruitless. So let's be partners. I will work your land and we'll split the crops right down the middle. It's an offer you cannot pass up."

What plan does the poor farmer have?

The rich landowner opened his eyes and yawned rudely.

"Which do you prefer, neighbor?" asked the hungry farmer. "The parts growing above or below the ground? I'll let you decide since it is your land. What'll it be?"

"What do I want?" the rich landowner asked drowsily. "Who would want the parts that grow below the ground? Of course I'll take the tops."

"Agreed!" said the farmer. "You just rest in the cool shade, and I'll get to work right away."

So the poor farmer tilled the soil until it was once again rich and fertile. He planted the seeds one-by-one. Each day he pulled the weeds and carefully watered the crops. The lazy landowner dozed and dreamed and snored.

Finally it was time to harvest the crops. The farmer announced loudly, "Neighbor, get up! Your farm has produced a bumper crop of potatoes, carrots, and onions and you get the tops!" The landowner woke just enough to see his pile of leafy tops. He was dumbfounded when he saw that the farmer was collecting the pile of potatoes, carrots, and onions.

"Wait a second here," complained the sleepy landowner. "You are taking the good parts, leaving me with just the leaves."

"Yes, indeed. It was your choice to take the parts above the ground." the farmer replied. "You're the boss."

How does the poor farmer trick the rich landowner?

"You have tricked me on my own farm! You plant this field again," ordered the landowner, "and this time I'll get the bottoms and you will be left with the parts growing above the soil."

"Agreed!" said the farmer as he raced home thinking of the rich stew he would make with his carefully grown potatoes, onions, and carrots.

The poor farmer worked the soil again. He planted more seeds, pulled the **pesky** weeds, and watered the crops while the lazy landowner dozed and dreamed and snored.

When it was time to harvest the crops, the farmer called from the fields, "Neighbor! Wake up, wake up! Your splendid farm has produced plenty of lettuce and cauliflower, and you wanted the parts growing beneath the soil this time."

The **slumbering** landowner opened one eye, observed his pile of dirty roots, and he glared at the farmer. "You have tricked me again! These bottoms are no good to eat!"

"Ah, but neighbor, that is what you requested. You wanted the bottoms of this harvest and you gave to me the parts that grow above the soil."

How does the farmer trick the landowner a second time?

"This is the last time you will trick me!" snarled the landowner. "You plant my fields again, and this time I will get both the tops and the bottoms."

"Agreed!" said the farmer. "You will get the tops and bottoms this time, neighbor." He ran off thinking about the delicious garden salad that he would have that evening.

The farmer returned to the field to cultivate the soil, plant the seeds, pull the weeds, and water the crops. He worked all season while the lazy landowner dozed and dreamed and snored.

Finally at harvest time, the farmer called out from the fields of high corn, "Neighbor, get up! You get both the tops and bottoms this time, and I'm left with just the middles."

The lazy landowner quickly woke to find dry corn shocks and hairy tassels in his pile. In a stunned silence, he watched the farmer carefully gather the tender ears of corn into another pile.

> How does the landowner get tricked a third time?

"You got what you asked for, Neighbor," explained the farmer. "You get the top tassels and the bottom shocks, and I get the middles. We agreed!"

Waving good-bye to the foolish landowner, the farmer, who was no longer poor and hungry, quickly left the farm with his wagon full of tender corn, crunchy cauliflower, crisp lettuce, fresh carrots, sweet onions, and russet potatoes.

The lazy landowner never slept through another harvest again.

Talking About the Story

- Ask students to describe how the farmer tricked the landowner three times. What lesson did the lazy landowner learn?

- Ask students if anyone has ever played a trick on them. Have them describe how they were tricked and what they learned from the experience.

Vocabulary in Action

Words From the Story

gentle

In the story gentle rains nourished the landowner's fertile land for many years. Someone or something that is gentle does not hurt anyone or anything else.

- Ask which would be gentle, a hurricane wind or a gentle breeze. Explain why.
- Have a student show how to act in a gentle way toward a plant, an animal, or another student.

pesky

The farmer plants seeds and pulls the pesky weeds. Something that keeps bothering you is pesky.

- Ask which insect can be pesky, a butterfly or a mosquito. Why do you think so?
- Have a pair of students act out a skit where one student is being pesky.

abundant

The landowner's harvest had always been abundant. When something is abundant, there is more than enough of it.

- Ask where water is abundant, in the ocean or in the desert. Explain.
- Call on a student to draw a picture of an abundant harvest of apples.

slumber

The landowner is always slumbering while the poor farmer works. When you slumber, you sleep very deeply.

- Ask which is the best place to slumber, in your bed or in your kitchen. Why?
- Ask students to pretend that they are slumbering.

Words About the Story

idle

The landowner spends his days idle. Someone or something that is idle is not moving or doing anything.

- Ask which is being idle, cleaning your room or lying on the beach. Explain why.
- Ask a student to sit and be idle in front of the class.

diligent

The poor but determined farmer is diligent about his work. If someone is diligent, they work very hard and very seriously.

- Ask who is being more diligent, someone who watches TV or someone who writes TV shows. Why?
- Ask students to show how a diligent student would act.

outsmart

The poor farmer outsmarted the rich landowner. When you outsmart someone, you trick them or beat them by doing something clever.

- Ask who is better at outsmarting others, a person who wins a contest by taking a shortcut or a person who wins by working harder. Why do you think so?
- Ask two students to perform a brief skit in which one student outsmarts the other.

Sheila's New Sweater

In this story a sheep named Sheila finds a stylish solution to a "woolly" problem.

Vocabulary

Words From the Story

These words appear in blue in the story. You might wish to go over their meanings briefly before reading the story.

perfect
If something is perfect, it could not be any better.

appreciate
If you appreciate something someone has done for you, you are pleased and would like to thank the person.

dreadful
If something is dreadful, it is so terrible that it could not be much worse.

scrawny
If someone is scrawny, they are so thin that they look like they might be sick.

Words About the Story

These words will be introduced after the story is read, using context from the story.

embarrass   **confidence**   **harsh**

Getting Ready for the Read-Aloud

Show students the picture on page 125 of the sheep holding a sweater. Read the title aloud, and ask students why a sheep might need to wear something other than a wool coat.

Tell students that some people suffer from allergies. Explain that an allergy can cause people to sneeze, to develop a rash, or to get sick if they smell, taste, or touch something to which they are allergic.

The following words occur in the story. They can be briefly explained as you come to them in the story: *shears*, a tool similar to a pair of scissors, but larger; *stethoscope*, an instrument used by a doctor to listen to sounds in a patient's body; *scampered*, ran quickly and happily.

Sheila's New Sweater

By Margaret Fetty

Illustrated by Vicki Bradley

Isn't she beautiful!" exclaimed Mrs. Woolrich. "Look at her four tiny hooves, little pink nose, and cute fluffy ears!"

"Yes, our little Sheila is **perfect**!" agreed Mr. Woolrich proudly. "Why, look how white her little fuzzy coat is!"

"I am sure it will be very thick, too," added Mrs. Woolrich. "Heavy, curly coats run in my family." Mrs. Woolrich leaned over and kissed her baby lamb.

"Bah-choo!" Sheila sneezed softly. Then she looked up at her parents and smiled.

As Sheila grew during the summer, her fuzzy coat turned into little curls. Miss Shearly, the wooldresser, would smile when she saw Sheila. "I'm going to have to sharpen my shears next spring," Miss Shearly exclaimed. "That lamb is going to have the thickest wool coat I've ever cut."

Mrs. Woolrich smiled widely and patted Sheila's head.

"Bah-choo!" sneezed Sheila. "Excuse me!"

Then one day late in the summer, Sheila was brushing her coat. "BAH-CHOO! BAH-CHOO!" Sheila sneezed.

Mrs. Woolrich looked into Sheila's bedroom. "Sheila, that is the third time you have sneezed this afternoon," she said. "In fact, you have been sneezing a lot this week. Are you catching a cold?"

Emphasize the *BAH* in Sheila's "sheepish" sneezes: *BAH-choo!* Use your voice to express Sheila's concern that her lambmates will laugh at her for losing her wool coat. Mrs. Woolrich's voice should show caring and concern as she reassures Sheila.

Why did Mrs. Woolrich think Sheila might have a cold?

"I hope not!" answered Sheila. She twisted her heavy white curls into a lambtail on top of her head. "Hoofball season is just starting. The Rams are playing the Colts out in the pasture tomorrow. I want to go watch the game with all my friends."

"Well, I think I will take you to visit Dr. Foldman just in case," responded Mrs. Woolrich. "Winter is coming, and you don't want to get sick."

Sheila liked to visit Dr. Foldman. He always had a smile for Sheila and gave big woolly hugs to make her feel better.

"Hello, Mrs. Woolrich! Hello, Sheila!" called Dr. Foldman when they entered the office. "What a wonderful surprise to see you two! What seems to be the problem?"

Mrs. Woolrich answered, "I think Sheila is getting a cold. She has been sneezing a lot lately."

"When did your sneezing start?" the doctor asked.

"Well, I noticed it about a week ago," Sheila said. "But I always seem to have a little tickle in my nose."

"Does your sneezing happen at a particular time?" questioned Dr. Foldman.

> Why do you think Dr. Foldman asked Sheila when she sneezed?

Sheila thought for a minute. "Well, since my wool is longer now, I seem to sneeze most often when I brush it."

Dr. Foldman looked closely at the skin under Sheila's wool coat. Next, he used a stethoscope to listen to Sheila breathe.

"Take a deep breath and bah out slowly," he instructed. Then, just as Dr. Foldman's arm passed near Sheila's nose, she began to sneeze, "BAH-CHOO! BAH-CHOO! BAH-CHOO! Excuse me!" Sheila exclaimed.

Dr. Foldman stepped back. "I think I know what the problem is," he announced. "I think that you are allergic to wool!"

> How did Dr. Foldman figure out that Sheila was allergic to wool?

"What!" gasped Sheila. "How can I be allergic to wool?"

"It doesn't happen too often," Dr. Foldman answered. "You have sensitive skin, Sheila. Your allergies will only get worse as your wool grows longer this winter."

"What does Sheila need to do to keep from getting worse?" asked Mrs. Woolrich.

"She needs to get sheared right away," answered Dr. Foldman.

Sheila looked so sad that Dr. Foldman gave her a hug. "BAH-CHOO! BAH-CHOO! BAH-CHOO!" sneezed Sheila. But Sheila was always polite. "Excuse me! And I do **appreciate** your help, Dr. Foldman. But this is one time the woolly hug doesn't make me feel any better," she said sadly.

> Why didn't Sheila feel better after a hug?

As Mrs. Woolrich and Sheila walked to the wooldresser's shop, Sheila became very worried. "This is **dreadful**! What am I going to do? All my lambmates will laugh at me if I don't wear my wool coat. Also, winter is coming. I'm going to freeze in such terribly cold weather!"

Mrs. Woolrich smiled at her little lamb and answered, "I'm not sure what to do yet, but there must be something! We just need to think."

Miss Shearly was very nice and suggested several fashionable coat styles that Sheila might like. Sheila decided to keep the lambtail on the top of her head. "After all," said Sheila, "the lambtail is not near my nose!"

> What are some possible solutions to Sheila's predicament?

Miss Shearly worked quickly. Before long, beautiful, white wool curls covered the floor around the chair. Sheila stood up with a shiver and bravely tried not to sniffle. When Sheila looked into the mirror, she saw a very **scrawny** sheep. "Everyone is going to laugh at me!" she cried.

Mrs. Woolrich had been looking through a magazine as she waited for Sheila, and one advertisement in particular caught her eye. She jumped up and gave Sheila a happy squeeze. Don't worry about what your lambmates will say, dear. I have an idea!"

> What do you think Mrs. Woolrich is going to do? Why do you think this?

On the way home, Sheila's mother stopped at the Farmer's Market. She bought a plant topped with big white puffs. It reminded Sheila of the puffs that she left lying on the floor of Miss Shearly's shop. Mrs. Woolrich also bought some red dye. "This will be just right," she smiled brightly. Sheila was puzzled, but when she asked her mother what she was doing, Mrs. Woolrich wisely answered, "Wool is just one way to stay warm."

Once at home, Mrs. Woolrich immediately set to work. She spun the puffs into long pieces of yarn. Then she soaked the yarn in the red dye. Next, Mrs. Woolrich got out her knitting needles and began to work. By the end of the night, Mrs. Woolrich had made a beautiful, red fluffy cotton sweater.

"It's beautiful!" gasped Sheila as she danced around the room. "It's much better than my white curly coat." Sheila happily pulled on the sweater. "And it's so warm, too! Thank you!"

Sheila couldn't wait to go to school the next morning. She woke up very early, hoofed down her breakfast, and scampered out the door. Once at school, Sheila walked into the classroom with her head held high.

> Why was Sheila excited about going to school?

"Wow, Sheila!" called Shelby, her best friend. "What a beautiful sweater! Where did you get it? It is so much prettier than my white coat!" All of Sheila's lambmates flocked around her and touched the sweater to feel its softness.

Sheila just smiled and politely said, "Thank you!" The other sheep didn't need to know about her allergies just yet. "BAH-CHOO! BAH-CHOO!" sneezed Sheila, when Shelby leaned a little too close. "Excuse me!" she said.

- Ask students to explain how Sheila's feelings about losing her wool coat changed throughout the story.
- Ask students to recall a time when they came up with a creative solution to a problem.

Vocabulary in Action

perfect

Sheila's parents say that their daughter and her fuzzy coat are perfect. If something is perfect, it could not be any better.

- Ask which might happen on a perfect day, losing your homework paper or winning first prize in a spelling bee. Why do you think so?
- Have students act out some perfect manners.

appreciate

Sheila appreciated the help Dr. Foldman gave her. If you appreciate something someone has done for you, you are pleased and would like to thank the person.

- Which would you appreciate, a cool drink on a hot day or extra homework? Why?
- Ask students to demonstrate how they would show that they appreciate a gift that someone has given them.

dreadful

Sheila thinks it is dreadful that she can't wear her wool coat any more. If something is dreadful, it is so terrible that it could not be much worse.

- Which would be dreadful, going out in the snow without shoes or without a sled? Why?
- Have students make faces as if they have just heard a dreadful sound.

scrawny

After Miss Shearly cut off Sheila's coat, Sheila looked scrawny. If someone is scrawny, they are so thin that they look like they might be sick.

- Ask which would make someone scrawny, not getting enough sleep or not eating enough food. Why do you think so?
- Call on a student to draw a scrawny puppy.

embarrass

Sheila felt embarrassed about losing her wool coat. When someone is embarrassed, they feel like they have done or said something that people think is wrong or silly.

- Which makes people feel embarrassed, making a silly mistake or making a new friend? Explain.
- Ask a student to act out feeling embarrassed about something.

confidence

By the end of the story, Sheila feels good about herself and her new sweater. Another way to say that is to say that she has confidence. If you have confidence, you feel good about yourself and are sure about how to do things.

- Ask which would give you more confidence, someone telling you that you did your work poorly or someone praising your work. Why?
- Call on a student to demonstrate how someone with a lot of confidence might walk.

harsh

Sheila worried that her lambmates might use harsh words and tease her about losing her wool. Something is harsh if it is rough and hurtful or can possibly cause damage.

- Ask which kind of weather is harsh, a storm with thunder and lightning or a gentle spring rainfall. Explain your answer.
- Call on a student to act as if someone had just said something harsh to him or her.

OWL MOON

In this narrative poem, a father and child go owling in the forest one snowy night.

Vocabulary

Words From the Poem

These words appear in blue in the poem. You might wish to go over their meanings briefly before reading the poem.

fade
To fade means to slowly become less bright or less strong.

disappointed
If you are disappointed, you are sad because something that you wanted did not happen.

thread
To thread something means to move it carefully and slowly through a narrow or winding space.

meadow
A meadow is a grassy field.

Words About the Poem

These words will be introduced after the poem is read, using context from the poem.

patience   **awe**   **anticipate**

Getting Ready for the Read-Aloud

Show students the picture on page 133 of the father and child walking in the snow at night. Read the title aloud and tell students that owls are usually active at night.

Explain that owls hunt for food when it is dark outside. They use their keen eyesight and hearing to find the fish, reptiles, and rabbits that they eat. Explain that the Great Horned Owl has a special call—"Whoo-whoo-who-who-who-whooooooo." You may want to show students a picture of the Great Horned Owl and have them try to imitate its call.

The following words occur in the poem. They can be briefly explained as you come to them in the poem: *owling*, looking for owls; *clearing*, an area of forest land without trees or brush.

OWL
MOON

By Jane Yolen
Illustrated by John Schoenherr

It was late one winter night,
long past my bedtime,
when Pa and I went owling.
There was no wind.
The trees stood still
as giant statues.
And the moon was so bright
the sky seemed to shine.
Somewhere behind us
a train whistle blew,
long and low,
like a sad, sad song.

I could hear it
through the woolen cap
Pa had pulled down
over my ears.
A farm dog answered the train,
and then a second dog
joined in.
They sang out,
trains and dogs,
for a real long time.
And when their voices
faded away
it was as quiet as a dream.
We walked on toward the woods,
Pa and I.

Our feet crunched
over the crisp snow
and little gray footprints
followed us.
Pa made a long shadow,
but mine was short and round.
I had to run after him
every now and then
to keep up,
and my short, round shadow
bumped after me.

Keep in mind that the poem is written from the child's point of view. Use a gentle voice to express the child's innocence and sense of wonder at this first owling experience. You may also want to perform the call of the Great Horned Owl.

But I never called out.
If you go owling
you have to be quiet,
that's what Pa always says.

Why do you have to be quiet when you go owling?

I had been waiting
to go owling with Pa
for a long, long time.

We reached the line
of pine trees,
black and pointy
against the sky,
and Pa held up his hand.
I stopped right where I was
and waited.
He looked up,
as if searching the stars,
as if reading a map up there.
The moon made his face
into a silver mask.

Then he called:
"*Whoo-whoo-who-who-who-whooooooo,*"
the sound of the Great Horned Owl.
"*Whoo-whoo-who-who-who-whooooooo.*"

Again he called out.
And then again.
After each call
he was silent
and for a moment we both listened.
But there was no answer.
Pa shrugged
and I shrugged.
I was not **disappointed**.
My brothers all said
sometimes there's an owl
and sometimes there isn't.

We walked on.
I could feel the cold,
as if someone's icy hand
was palm-down on my back.
And my nose
and the tops of my cheeks
felt cold and hot
at the same time.
But I never said a word.
If you go owling
you have to be quiet
and make your own heat.

We went into the woods.
The shadows
were the blackest things
I had ever seen.
They stained the white snow.
My mouth felt furry,
for the scarf over it
was wet and warm.
I didn't ask
what kinds of things
hide behind black trees

in the middle of the night.
When you go owling
you have to be brave.

Why do you have to be brave when you go owling?

Then we came to a clearing
in the dark woods.
The moon was high above us.
It seemed to fit exactly
over the center of the clearing
and the snow below it
was whiter than the milk in a
cereal bowl.

I sighed
and Pa held up his hand
at the sound.
I put my mittens
over the scarf
over my mouth
and listened hard.
And then Pa called:
"*Whoo-whoo-who-who-who-whooooooo.*
Whoo-whoo-who-who-who-whoooooooo."
I listened
and looked so hard
my ears hurt
and my eyes got cloudy
with the cold.
Pa raised his face
to call out again,
but before he could
open his mouth
an echo
came **threading** its way
through the trees.
"*Whoo-whoo-who-who-who-whooooooo.*"

Pa almost smiled.
Then he called back:
"*Whoo-whoo-who-who-who-
whooooooo,*"
just as if he
and the owl
were talking about supper
or about the woods
or the moon
or the cold.
I took my mitten
off the scarf
off my mouth,
and I almost smiled, too.

The owl's call came closer
from high up in the trees
on the edge of the **meadow**.
Nothing in the meadow moved.
All of a sudden
an owl shadow,
part of the big tree shadow,
lifted off
and flew right over us.
We watched silently
with heat in our mouths,
the heat of all those words
we had not spoken.
The shadow hooted again.

Pa turned on
his big flashlight
and caught the owl
just as it was landing
on a branch.

For one minute,
three minutes,
maybe even a hundred minutes,
we stared at one another.

Then the owl
pumped its great wings
and lifted off the branch

like a shadow
without sound.
It flew back into the forest.
"Time to go home,"
Pa said to me.
I knew then I could talk,
I could even laugh out loud.
But I was a shadow
as we walked home.

When you go owling
you don't need words
or warm
or anything but hope.
That's what Pa says.
The kind of hope
that flies
on silent wings
under a shining
Owl Moon.

Talking About the Poem

- Ask students to describe the things that you must do when you go owling.
- Ask students if they have ever seen an owl or other interesting bird. Have them describe what the bird looked like and how it acted.

Vocabulary in Action

fade

The sounds of trains and dogs barking faded away as the child and the father move deeper into the woods. To fade means to slowly become less bright or less strong.

- Ask which fades, the color of blue jeans or the color of orange juice. Why do you think so?
- Have a student imitate a train sound that gradually fades away.

thread

The sound of the owl's call came threading through the forest. To thread something means to move it carefully and slowly through a narrow or winding space.

- Ask which you might thread, a lump of clay to make a bowl or a wire through some beads to make a necklace. Explain why.
- Have a student show what it would look like to thread a string through large beads.

disappointed

The child is not disappointed when they do not hear an owl at first. If you are disappointed, you are sad because something that you wanted did not happen.

- Ask which might make someone disappointed, not being able to go to recess or not being able to go to the dentist. Why?
- Call on students to show what they might say or do when they are disappointed for some reason, such as when a special trip or event is canceled.

meadow

The owl's call came from the edge of the meadow. A meadow is a grassy field.

- Ask which you might be likely to find in a meadow, a mouse or a crab. Why?
- Ask students to act out what they would do for fun in a meadow.

Words About the Poem

patience

The child knew that you must have patience when you go owling. If you have patience, you are able to wait for something that takes a long time.

- Would a boy need more patience to ride his bike to the park two blocks away or to help a young child learn to tie her shoes? Explain your answer.
- Have two students act out a scene in which one student shows patience and the other does not.

awe

The father and child are in awe of the owl. Awe is what you feel when you see something that is so great you think it cannot be true.

- Ask which might cause someone to feel awe, seeing a sunset or seeing a stop sign. Why do you think this?
- Call on a student to pretend that he or she is in awe of something he or she has seen.

anticipate

The father and child anticipate seeing an owl in the woods. When you anticipate something, you look forward to it happening and you are excited about it.

- Ask which would you anticipate, doing your chores or going to a party. Why?
- Have a student act like someone who is anticipating a day at the beach.

The Dream Collector

In this story a boy helps out a strange visitor who makes one of the boy's dreams comes true.

Vocabulary

Words From the Story

These words appear in blue in the story. You might wish to go over their meanings briefly before reading the story.

disaster
A disaster is when something very bad happens.

overrun
When a place is overrun by something, like animals, it means that there are a large number of them there.

variety
A variety is many different kinds of something.

magnificent
Something that is magnificent is very good, very beautiful, or very special in some way.

Words About the Story

These words will be introduced after the story is read, using context from the story.

pursue **bizarre** **imaginative**

Getting Ready for the Read-Aloud

Show students the picture on page 139 of Zachary and the Dream Collector. Read the title aloud and tell students that a collector is a person who gathers interesting things.

Explain to students that this story has elements of fantasy. Although the characters seem like real people, the plot includes some events that could not happen in real life. The author uses imagination to create a story about what happens to dreams when people wake up in the morning.

Briefly introduce some words that may be unfamiliar to students: *regulations*, rules; *piston*, a part of a car engine; *spark plug*, small object in a car engine that creates sparks to burn fuel; *socket set*, set of tools that are used to turn bolts.

The Dream Collector

By Troon Harrison
Illustrated by Alan and Lea Daniel

Quite early, before anyone else was awake, Zachary saw that it was going to be an extraordinary Saturday. Two zebras and a huge shaggy dog were drinking from the birdbath. Zachary had been asking his parents for months if he could have a dog like that.

"Wait for me!" he shouted, pulling on his sneakers.

The zebras galloped away through the flowers when Zachary opened the door. The dog chased after them. As Zachary started to follow he noticed another unusual thing. At the end of his driveway was a truck with dusty fenders. A short man was standing on a crate, looking under the hood. He wore overalls with shiny buttons.

Use your voice and mannerisms to express the matter-of-fact attitude of the Dream Collector. Your inflection might also reflect Zachary's amazement at the extraordinary situation in which he finds himself.

Why did Zachary think it was going to be an extraordinary Saturday?

"Good morning," said Zachary. "Who are you?"

"Read the door panel," suggested the man with a chuckle.

"Dream Collector. Streets Clear by Dawn." Zachary read the lettering aloud. "What does that mean?" he wondered.

The Dream Collector pulled his head out from under the hood and smiled. He had cheeks the color of old plums and eyes as blue as summer afternoons. "Have you ever thought about what happens to your dreams?" he asked Zachary.

Zachary shook his head.

"You haven't? Well, I come around at dawn and collect them. It's city regulations," the Dream Collector explained.

"Wow! What happens if you don't collect the dreams?" asked Zachary.

"That would be a **disaster**!" exclaimed the Dream Collector. "The closer it gets to morning, the more real the dreams become. Once sunlight touches them, they're here to stay. Imagine! The whole neighborhood would be **overrun** with dreams!"

Who is the man at the end of Zachary's driveway? What job does he do?

At that moment two pirates strolled down the driveway.

"Were they someone's dream?" asked Zachary.

"Yes," replied the Dream Collector as he poked his head back under the hood.

Zachary heard him mutter something about piston rings. "Is your truck broken down?" he asked.

"It is. It won't start and I've forgotten my toolbox." The Dream Collector sounded worried.

"I can get some tools," offered Zachary. "What do you need?"

"Can you find a spark-plug wrench, a battery tester and a socket set?"

Zachary ran into the garage and looked at his dad's tools. He wasn't too sure what some of them were called. He took a **variety** so the Dream Collector could choose the one he needed.

Why is Zachary looking for tools?

Just as Zachary reached the truck, the shaggy dog dashed by chasing three rabbits. "Hey, that dog was *my* dream!" exclaimed Zachary in astonishment. "I wish I had a dog like that."

By now there were dreams everywhere. The Dream Collector looked around anxiously. "The street should be clear already," he moaned. "Soon the sun will be up. This is serious. Maybe you can do another special job for me."

Why is the Dream Collector feeling anxious?

"What?" asked Zachary.

"Perhaps you can load the dreams into the truck. Some dreams, like dogs, might be hard to catch though," he said, with a twinkle in his eye. "Do you think you can do it?"

"Oh yes, I can do that," Zachary said proudly.

Zachary crept into the house and carefully chose the things he'd need to catch the dreams. When he came back out the sun was rising. He would have to move fast.

Now the yard was crowded with dreams.

"Follow me everyone!" Zachary called, leading the way.

One by one, the dreams climbed the ramp into the truck. Zachary gave a sigh of relief. Only the dog was still missing.

Zachary walked down the street again, whistling for it. The dog barked from somewhere in the bushes.

"Come on out!" called Zachary, pushing aside branches. But the dog had disappeared.

How did Zachary help the Dream Collector?

Sunlight was shining on the front windows of all the houses. Zachary went to tell the Dream Collector that one dream was still on the loose.

"Stand back!" warned the Dream Collector when Zachary appeared. "I'm going to try starting the truck."

Zachary stepped out of the way. There was a long pause. The knight's horse neighed. Then the engine burst into life with a **magnificent** roar. It was just in time. Sunlight was flooding the street.

"Hurrah!" shouted the Dream Collector. "Thanks for your help. I couldn't have managed without you!"

"I can't find the dog!" called Zachary.

The Dream Collector gave a piercing whistle and the shaggy dog bounded from the bushes. It looked exactly the way Zachary thought a dog should look, with a drooping mustache and eyes like chocolate kisses. When the dog wagged its tail its hind feet almost lifted off the ground.

What do you think will happen to the dog?

"Think you'd like this dog?" asked the Dream Collector.

"I'd love this dog," replied Zachary.

"Then it's yours," said the Dream Collector.

Zachary let out a whoop. He could hardly believe his luck. "Thank you!" he shouted.

Zachary took his wonderful, dream-come-true dog by the collar, and together they ran up the driveway.

"Let's go and jump on Mom and Dad's bed," Zachary said. "They will think they're still dreaming when they wake up and see *you*!"

Talking About the Story

- Ask students to summarize the story by describing the Dream Collector's problem and telling how Zachary helped him solve it.

- Invite students to tell what would happen if one of the characters from their dreams showed up in their real life.

Vocabulary in Action

disaster

In the story, the Dream Collector said it would be a disaster if he didn't collect the dreams. A disaster is when something very bad happens.

- Which would be a disaster, spilt milk or a big flood. Why do you think so?
- Have students tell what they would do if there was a disaster in their neighborhood.

overrun

The Dream Collector said the neighborhood would be overrun with dreams if he didn't collect them. When a place is overrun by something, like animals, it means that there are a large number of them there.

- Ask which might overrun a pond, frogs or rabbits. Explain what you mean.
- Ask students to act out what would happen if the classroom were overrun with mice.

magnificent

The truck engine made a magnificent roar. Something that is magnificent is very good, very beautiful, or very special in some way.

- Ask which is more likely to be magnificent, a sunset or a pebble. Why?
- Invite a volunteer to act like a king or queen wearing a magnificent robe.

variety

Zachary took a variety of tools to the Dream Collector. A variety is many different kinds of something.

- Ask students which would have variety, a box of crayons or a box of corn flakes. Why do you think that?
- Ask a volunteer to gather a variety of classroom objects.

Words About the Story

pursue

Zachary ran after the dog to try to catch it. Another way to say that is to say that Zachary pursued the dog. If you pursue someone, you follow them, usually to try to catch them.

- Ask which you might pursue, a hat that has blown off your head or a kite on a windy day. Explain why.
- Have one student pursue another safely around the classroom.

bizarre

The idea of someone who collects dreams and puts them in a truck is very unusual. Another way to say that is that the idea of a Dream Collector is bizarre. Something bizarre is very strange.

- Ask which would be bizarre, a talking bird or a talking horse. Explain your answer.
- Challenge students to make up a bizarre story or song.

imaginative

The author of this story had a very interesting idea about dreams. Another way to say that is to say that the author was very imaginative. Someone who is imaginative often has very creative and interesting ideas.

- Ask which is more imaginative, memorizing a poem that you read or writing an original poem. Why do you think so?
- Ask students to write an imaginative poem.

Jane Goodall

This selection tells the real-life story of a woman who lived among chimpanzees and studied their behavior.

Vocabulary

Words From the Story

These words appear in blue in the story. You might wish to go over their meanings briefly before reading the story.

excel
If you excel at something, you do it better than most other people.

industrious
If you are industrious, you work very hard and get a lot done.

remote
A remote place is far away from where people live.

accompany
When you accompany someone, you go somewhere with them.

gesture
When you move your hands or your body to help people understand what you are saying, you make a gesture.

Words About the Story

These words will be introduced after the story is read, using context from the story.

reveal   **conserve**

Getting Ready for the Read-Aloud

Show students the picture on page 146 of Jane Goodall and the chimpanzee. Read the title aloud. Tell students that this is a true story of a woman who spent years in Africa living among chimpanzees and studying their behavior.

Ask students to look closely at the chimpanzee shown on page 146. Explain that chimpanzees are a kind of ape and that they live in Africa. Point out that adult chimps are about 4 feet tall. Have students compare the animal's size to their own.

Briefly introduce some words that may be unfamiliar to students: *game warden,* a worker who takes care of animals in a state or national forest; *binoculars,* a pair of special glasses that makes things far away look close; *termites,* insects that live in hot places and eat wood; *sanctuaries,* areas of land where wildlife is kept safe.

Jane Goodall

Bringing the Story to Life

Hiking through a wild forest in Africa, Jane Goodall followed a chimpanzee she'd named David Greybeard. He swung from tree to tree over her head. Then Jane became tangled in vines and was sure she had lost the chimp. When she came to a clearing in the forest, she was surprised to see David again. He was sitting by the edge of a stream and seemed to be waiting for her.

Display pictures of African rain forests in the area where students will gather to hear the selection. Ask students to look at these pictures and imagine being in the setting as you read. If possible, also play an audiotape of rain forest sounds or download a free rain forest screensaver with sounds onto your computer screen.

What was Jane doing? Why do you think she was doing that?

Jane Goodall was born in London, England, in 1934. Jane **excelled** in school, especially in the subjects that she enjoyed. Her favorite subject of study, however, was the animal world. By the time Jane was 18, she was determined to go to Africa to work with animals. Every day she wondered when she would be able to go. Every day she dreamed about what she would do when she finally got there.

Jane Goodall was 23 when she first sailed to Africa. Her first job there was helping the well-known archaeologists Dr. Louis Leakey and his wife Mary hunt for fossils and ancient bones. They were learning about the past by studying modern animals and early humans.

After a trip to Kenya, Dr. Leakey became fascinated with chimpanzees. He decided to send Jane to Gombe National Park in Tanzania to learn all she could about chimps. Jane had no training as a scientist, but she was very intelligent and **industrious**. Because of this, Dr. Leakey felt Jane was the perfect person for the job.

Jane went back to England to study and prepare for her trip. She read everything she could about chimps and worked at the London Zoo. Finally, when she was 26, she was ready to return to Africa and begin her work. Gombe National Park was in a **remote** part of Africa, however, and the government felt that it was dangerous for a young woman to be there alone. Therefore, Jane asked her mother to go with her and help her with her work.

What were the clues that Jane would be a success at her work?

Jane and her mother's first night in Gombe was beautiful. As she recalled, "By the time I lay down to sleep in my camp bed under the twinkling stars, I already felt that I belonged in this new forest world, that this is where I was meant to be."

Jane faced many challenges in her first months in Gombe. At first, Jane had to hike in the forests **accompanied** by scouts. The noise she and the scouts made caused the chimps to run away. Jane persevered, however, and the game warden finally let her hike alone. Being alone allowed her to get closer to the chimps. Using binoculars, she watched the chimps and learned about their way of life.

She observed the chimps silently day after day. It took a very long time for the chimps to become comfortable enough with her to stay close. About fifty chimps lived near the camp. After awhile, Jane realized that each chimp had its own look and personality. When she could recognize each chimp, she gave each one a name.

What challenges did Jane face during her first months in Gombe?

One day Jane watched a chimp that she had named David Greybeard. David hunted and killed a small animal, and then shared his kill with other chimps. Jane had made an important discovery. Before that time scientists did not know that chimps knew how to hunt. They had also believed that chimps did not eat meat.

Something else suprising happened. David Greybeard visited Jane's camp! David Greybeard came back to camp day after day. Before long, other chimps were joining David Greybeard on his camp visits. Jane's patience had paid off. She was finally able to get as close to the chimps as she wanted.

David Greybeard also provided Jane with her most exciting discovery. One morning, Jane saw David poking a blade of grass into a termite mound. When he pulled it out, it was covered in termites. David picked the termites off of the grass with his lips and ate them. David had used the blade of grass as a tool to get the termites out of the mound. Up until this moment, scientists thought that only humans used tools.

What surprising things did Jane learn about chimps?

As the chimps learned to relax around people, both local residents and students from around the world came to help Jane with her research. They made many other discoveries about the chimps' behavior, such as how they use **gestures** and calls to communicate. Chimps use about thirty different calls to send messages to one another. In addition, chimps hug, kiss, hold hands, and pat one another on the back. These gestures appear to mean almost the same things to chimps as they do to humans.

Chimps also spend a lot of time playing with their friends. When chimps play, they tickle or chase one another, and they like to wrestle. During quieter moments, chimps often sit very close and groom one another. They do this for many reasons. One chimp might be removing small insects from another's fur, or he might be trying to calm his friend after a bad scare.

Jane recorded what she had learned during her twenty-five-year study of chimps in a book titled *The Chimpanzees of Gombe*. This book was published in 1986. Jane's work continued to grow and change as she realized that there were many animals all over Africa that needed her help.

Jane Goodall died in 2003, and her work continues in the hands of the people she inspired. In the last years of her life, Jane worked with people all over the world to find ways to protect chimpanzees and other animals. She used donations to set up sanctuaries that would protect animals from harm. Above all, she encouraged people all over the world to be kind to both people and animals.

Talking About the Story

- Ask students to summarize what Jane Goodall learned about chimps.
- Invite students to name a pet or wild animal that they have watched closely. Encourage students to tell what they learned about the animal from watching it.

Vocabulary in Action

excel

Jane excelled in school, especially in the subjects she enjoyed. If you excel at something, you do it better than most other people.

- Ask which might help you excel at school, working hard or wearing nice clothes. Explain why.
- Have students act out something that they excel at doing.

industrious

Jane was intelligent and industrious. If you are industrious, you work very hard and get a lot done.

- Ask which an industrious student might do, finish her homework as soon as she gets home or put off doing her homework. Why do you think so?
- Have groups of students create skits in which at least one character acts in an industrious way.

gesture

Jane discovered how chimps gesture to each other. When you move your hands or your body to help people understand what you are saying, you make a gesture.

- Ask when you would be more likely to use gestures, when it is light outside or when it is too dark to see. Why?
- Encourage students to make an appropriate gesture as they join you in saying: *Look to the left.*

Words About the Story

reveal

Jane wrote a book to reveal what she learned about chimps. When you reveal something, you show it to people for the first time.

- Ask which you might reveal to a classmate, a new outfit or your old sneakers. Why?
- Put a small object in a box. Ask a volunteer to open the box and reveal what is inside.

remote

The park where Jane worked was in a remote place. A remote place is far away from where people live.

- Ask which you would find in a remote area, lots of wild plants or lots of small farms. Explain.
- Draw a circle on the board. Have a volunteer draw simple houses on one side of the circle. Then have the volunteer point to the remote side of the circle where there are no houses.

accompany

When she first started to work, Jane was accompanied by others. When you accompany someone, you go somewhere with them.

- Ask when you would be more likely to be accompanied by others, when you are brushing your teeth or when you are eating lunch at school. Explain.
- Ask a student to invite another student to accompany him or her on a school errand.

conserve

Jane set up sanctuaries to conserve animals. When you conserve something, you save it from being used up or destroyed.

- Ask which you would want to conserve, clean water or dirty water. Explain.
- Ask a few volunteers to do jumping jacks. Then ask them to show how they would conserve their energy.

EAT-IT-ALL ELAINE

In this poem a quiet yet comical camper causes a stir by acting out her well-deserved nickname.

Vocabulary

Words From the Poem

These words appear in blue in the poem. You might wish to go over their meanings briefly before reading the poem.

arrival
When you get to the place where you were going, you have made your arrival.

stroll
If you stroll somewhere, you walk in a slow and calm way.

command
If you are in command, you are in charge of a group of people or a situation.

banquet
A banquet is a meal with a lot of fancy food.

outstanding
A person or thing that is outstanding shows that it is special in some way.

Words About the Poem

These words will be introduced after the poem is read, using context from the poem.

peers   **amusing**

Getting Ready for the Read-Aloud

Show students the picture on pages 152 and 153 of Elaine and her fellow campers. Read the title aloud, and explain that you will be reading a poem about a girl named Elaine who has a very curious habit. Have students use the picture and title to predict what the poem might be about.

Explain that kids who go to summer camp do lots of fun activities, such as swimming, hiking, horseback riding, and crafts. Point out that this poem is about a camp in Maine. Help students find Maine on a map.

EAT-IT-ALL ELAINE

By Kaye Starbird

Illustrated by Amy Wummer

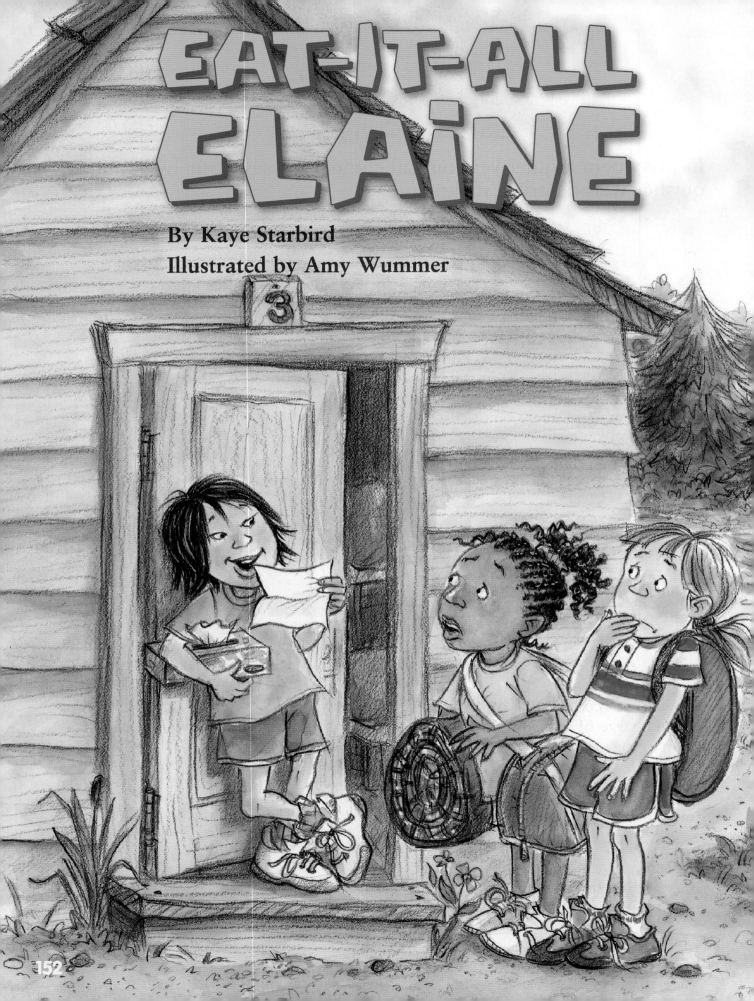

went away last August
    To summer camp in Maine,
And there I met a camper
Called Eat-it-all Elaine.
Although Elaine was quiet,
She liked to cause a stir
By acting out the nickname
Her camp-mates gave to her.

The day of our **arrival**
At Cabin Number Three
When girls kept coming over
To greet Elaine and me,
She took a piece of Kleenex
And calmly chewed it up,
Then **strolled** outside the cabin
And ate a buttercup.

What unusual things did
Elaine do on her first day
at camp?

Elaine, from that day forward,
Was always in **command**.
On hikes, she'd eat some birch-bark
On swims, she'd eat some sand.
At meals, she'd swallow prune-pits
And never have a pain,
While everyone around her
Would giggle, "Oh, Elaine!"

What kinds of things did
Elaine do that fit
her nickname?

One morning, berry-picking,
A bug was in her pail,
And though we thought for certain
Her appetite would fail,
Elaine said, "Hmm, a stinkbug."

And while we murmured, "Ooh,"
She ate her pail of berries
And ate the stinkbug, too.

Were you surprised that
Elaine ate the stinkbug?
Why or why not?

The night of Final **Banquet**
When counselors were handing
Awards to different children
Whom they believed **outstanding**,
To every *thinking* person
At summer camp in Maine
The Most Outstanding Camper
Was Eat-it-all Elaine.

Talking About the Poem

- Ask students to describe some of the things Elaine did to deserve The Most Outstanding Camper award.

- Invite students to think of some things they like to do and come up with silly nicknames for themselves.

Vocabulary in Action

Words From the Poem

arrival

In the story the other campers greeted Elaine on the day of their arrival at Cabin Number Three. When you get to the place where you were going, you have made your arrival.

- Ask students when they would make an arrival, at the end of a movie or at the beginning of a school day. Explain why.
- Have students leave the classroom and then act out their arrival to the group.

command

Elaine was always in command at camp. If you are in command, you are in charge of a group of people or situation.

- Ask which person might be in command, a tour guide at the museum or a visitor at a hospital. Why do you think so?
- Have students work in pairs and take turns giving simple commands and carrying them out.

Words About the Poem

peers

All of the campers enjoyed the same kinds of activities. Another way to say that is to say the campers are peers. Your peers are the people who are equal to you because they are the same age or do the same things.

- Ask students which group of people would be their peers, their grandparents or the students in another third grade class. Explain your answer.
- Have students list things to do with their peers.

stroll

Elaine strolled outside the cabin and ate a buttercup. If you stroll somewhere, you walk in a slow and calm way.

- Ask in which situation you would stroll, looking at animals in the zoo or trying to make it to school on time. Why?
- Have students stroll from one side of the classroom to the other.

banquet

Camp counselors handed out awards on the night of the final banquet. A banquet is a meal with a lot of fancy food.

- Ask which would be a banquet, a Thanksgiving dinner or a neighborhood picnic. Explain your answer.
- Have students plan menus for their "dream" banquet.

outstanding

Elaine receives The Most Outstanding Camper award at the Final Banquet. A person or thing that is outstanding shows that it is special in some way.

- Ask which animal would be outstanding, a dog that can jump through a hoop or a dog that can bark. Explain why.
- Have each student name something about themselves that makes them outstanding.

amusing

Everybody liked Eat-It-All Elaine because she was funny and did some unusual things. Another way to say this is to say Elaine was amusing. Something is amusing if you enjoy it and it holds your attention.

- Ask which would be more amusing, a book about a dog who ran for president or a diary entry written by George Washington on the day he was elected president. Why do you think so?
- Ask volunteers to tell an amusing joke or riddle.

SAM THE ZAMBONI MAN

This story tells how Sam, the driver of a Zamboni, shares his love for hockey with his grandson Matt.

Vocabulary

Words From the Story

These words appear in blue in the story. You might wish to go over their meanings briefly before reading the story.

glisten
To glisten means to shine from being wet or oily.

glide
To glide means to move smoothly and easily.

steer
When you steer something, such as a car, you control it so that it goes in the direction that you want it to.

gloomy
If something is gloomy, it is so dark and empty that it makes you feel sad.

entire
If something is entire, it is whole.

Words About the Story

These words will be introduced after the story is read, using context from the story.

tradition   **wisdom**

Getting Ready for the Read-Aloud

Show students the picture on pages 158 and 159 of Matt watching his grandfather make a hockey goal. Read the title aloud, and tell children that *Zamboni* is the name of a machine that scrapes and smoothes the ice at a skating rink.

Explain that Matt's grandfather, who was once a hockey player, still loves the sport. Though he can no longer play, he is still able to work at a hockey stadium and enjoy the game as a spectator. He also is eager to share everything he knows about hockey with his grandson.

The following words occur in the story. They can be briefly explained as you come to them in the story: *rink*, a large, smooth surface for ice or roller skating; *puck*, a small, hard rubber disk that is moved across the ice in ice hockey; *period*, a timed section of an event.

SAM THE ZAMBONI MAN

By James Stevenson
Illustrated by Harvey Stevenson

Matt lived in the country. He'd seen kids play hockey on the pond behind his school, but he'd never been to a real hockey game in the city.

One day he got a letter from his grandpa. "Come to the city for a visit, Matt," said the letter, "and we'll go to a hockey game together."

Matt's grandpa worked at a huge stadium. He drove the Zamboni—the big blue-and-white machine that rolled around the rink, melting and scraping and smoothing the ice.

People called him Sam the Zamboni Man. "Can I go to Grandpa's?" Matt asked his parents. "I want to see a hockey game and watch Grandpa drive the Zamboni."

Bringing the Story to Life

Use your voice to convey the warm and loving relationship that Matt and his grandfather have. Also emphasize the many descriptive details about hockey that bring this story to life.

His parents said yes.

Why did Matt want to visit his grandpa?

Matt's grandpa took him to a hockey game on the first night of his visit. They went into the stadium and bought a box of Cracker Jack to share. There was a big crowd, but their seats were very close to the rink, and Matt could see everything that happened. A friend of Grandpa's had cleared the ice, so it was **glistening** when the game began.

Matt loved watching the players in bright uniforms zoom by at top speed, chasing the small black puck. He loved the sound of skates scraping, and hockey sticks clattering and smacking, and the way the crowd yelled and cheered and jumped to its feet.

Near the end of the first period Matt's grandpa said, "I have to go to work now. Will you sit right here and wait until I come back?"

"Sure, Grandpa," said Matt.

A few minutes later a loud buzzer sounded, and the hockey teams skated off the ice. It was the end of the first period. Music began to play over the loudspeaker. Then, from the far end of the rink, the blue-and-white Zamboni came rolling slowly out onto the ice. Matt's grandpa was at the wheel.

When his grandpa went by, Matt waved. His grandpa waved back. Matt felt very proud. He felt as if all the people in the stadium knew that Sam was his grandpa.

What did Sam's grandpa do at the end of the first period?

When the game was over, Matt went with his grandpa to a room under the stands where the Zamboni was kept. He helped his grandpa wash and polish the Zamboni. When it was all shined up, Grandpa said, "Are you getting sleepy, Matt?"

"Oh, no," said Matt. "I'm not sleepy at all."

"Well, then," said Grandpa, "maybe I'll just put on my skates for a few minutes."

Grandpa went to a battered green locker and took out an old pair of hockey skates. The laces had been broken so many times that they were mostly knots. But Grandpa put the skates on and tied them up. From the back of the locker he took a splintery hockey stick that was bandaged with black tape.

He picked up a chipped puck from the floor and went out to the rink. Matt followed.

"Were you a hockey player, Grandpa, when you were young?" asked Matt.

"Yes, when I was young, Matt," said Grandpa. "A long time ago."

The stadium was dark now. There was only a single light hanging over the rink. Matt watched as his grandpa **glided** out onto the ice and began to skate, **steering** the puck ahead of him.

Grandpa's shadow made long shapes as he sailed around the rink. The only sound was the scratching of skate blades. Back and forth Grandpa skated, the puck always ahead of him. Suddenly he stopped, sending a shower of ice into the air. Then he started again, skating faster and faster toward the goal. He drew back his stick. WHACK! The puck flew into the net.

Matt clapped and cheered. His grandpa raised his stick in the air and waved to Matt, grinning. Then he turned and waved to the rows and rows of empty seats.

Why do you think Matt's grandpa waved to the rows of empty seats?

"Who were you waving to, Grandpa?" asked Matt.

"Oh, I thought maybe I heard some cheering," said Grandpa. "Guess I was wrong." He laughed.

"I was cheering," said Matt.

"I *know* you were," said Grandpa, and he gave Matt a hug.

On the last night of Matt's visit Grandpa asked, "Would you like to go to the stadium again tonight?"

"Can we?" said Matt. "I'd really like that."

But when they got there, the stadium was closed.

"I guess there isn't any game tonight," said Matt. He was really disappointed, but he didn't want his grandpa to know.

"It doesn't matter, Grandpa," he said. "I've had lots of fun."

"So have I, Matt," said his grandpa. "Let's go in, anyway." He took a key out of his pocket and unlocked a side door. They stood looking down over the dark, empty seats. The stadium was very still and **gloomy** looking.

"Let's go home, Grandpa," said Matt.

"Wait here just a minute," said Grandpa.

Matt waited while his grandpa ran down the stairs and disappeared.

Suddenly lights began to come on, first above some seats, then above others, then above the rink itself. Now the whole stadium was bright, and the ice sparkled. Music began to play over the loudspeaker, and a booming voice said, "Good evening, ladies and gentlemen, and welcome to the stadium!"

Matt recognized his grandpa's voice right away.

"Tonight," said the voice, "we have a very special treat. The Zamboni will be driven by the youngest Zamboni driver of all time. Come on down, Matt!"

Whose voice came over the loudspeaker? What did the voice say?

Matt began to laugh and ran down the steps just as the Zamboni came out onto the ice.

His grandpa got down and lifted Matt onto the Zamboni. Then he climbed back on and sat Matt on his lap. Matt held the wheel. He felt very high in the air, looking down on the rink. It was almost scary.

"Ready to roll, Matt?" said his grandpa.

"What do I do, Grandpa?" asked Matt. There were a lot of levers and gearshifts.

"Just steer, that's all," said his grandpa, and the Zamboni began to roll forward. "Here we go!"

Matt held the wheel steady. After a while he tried turning it a little bit to the right. The Zamboni went to the right. He turned the wheel to the left. The Zamboni swung to the left. Matt steered the Zamboni in a big loop. And another big loop. Then a figure eight. Then a zigzag back.

Matt was laughing now, and so was his grandpa. It was the most fun Matt had ever had. He covered the ice with circles and swirls and loops.

He tried to write a gigantic G for *Grandpa*. It didn't look perfect, but then he wrote an M for *Matt*, and that one was pretty good. Matt ended by zigzagging all the way down the **entire** rink.

Then he steered the Zamboni carefully out the gate and back to its room under the stands.

"That was great, Grandpa," said Matt on the way home. "Can we do it again next year if I come to visit?"

What did his grandpa let Matt do with the Zamboni?

"I think we may be too busy to spend time driving the Zamboni," said Grandpa.

"Why?" said Matt.

"Because next year, when you come to visit, I'll be teaching you how to skate and how to play hockey. Would you like that, Matt?"

"Yes, I would," said Matt. "*A lot.*"

"So would I," said Grandpa, and they both laughed.

Talking About the Story

- Ask students to describe some things that Matt does with his grandpa at the hockey rink.
- Ask students what special things they have done with a grandparent or a close relative. Encourage them to share some of their experiences with the class.

Vocabulary in Action

glisten

The ice on the hockey rink is glistening when the game starts. To glisten means to shine from being wet or oily.

- Ask which would make your skin glisten, rubbing it with baby oil or sprinkling powder on it. Why is this so?
- Have students use glitter to make a picture that shows something glistening.

gloomy

The hockey stadium looks gloomy when no one is there. If something is gloomy, it is so dark and empty that it makes you feel sad.

- Ask which would be gloomy, a school auditorium late at night or a swimming pool on a sunny summer afternoon. Why is this so?
- Ask students to make a face as if they were in a gloomy mood.

glide

Matt watches as his grandpa glides out onto the ice, driving the Zamboni. To glide means to move smoothly and easily.

- Ask students which they might glide better on, a polished floor or a sandy beach. Why?
- Call on a student to imitate someone gliding on a sidewalk on roller or in-line skates.

steer

Matt's grandpa steers the puck ahead of him. When you steer something, such as a car, you control it so that it goes in the direction that you want it to.

- Ask which you might not be able steer, a boat or a house. Explain your answer.
- Have students act out steering a bicycle along a steep, winding, downhill path.

entire

Matt drove the Zamboni back and forth across the entire rink. If something is entire, it is whole.

- Ask which would be more to eat, half a pizza or an entire pizza. Why is that?
- Call on a student to walk around the entire classroom.

tradition

It is a tradition at hockey games for the announcer to welcome the fans. A tradition is something that a group of people always does to celebrate a special time.

- Ask which is a popular tradition for fans at sporting events, singing our national anthem or reading a book during the game. Why?
- Call on a student to talk about a tradition in which he or she participates.

wisdom

Matt's grandpa has a lot of wisdom about the game of hockey. Wisdom is what you learn from things that happen to you during your life.

- Ask who might have more wisdom about life, an 80-year-old woman or a 10-year-old girl. Why do you think so?
- Working in pairs, have one student share a bit of wisdom while his or her partner demonstrates how to listen carefully when someone is saying something important.

Donavan's Word Jar

Why would someone want to collect words? In this story a boy not only collects words but also finds a very unusual way to use his collection.

Vocabulary

Words From the Story

These words appear in blue in the story. You might wish to go over their meanings briefly before reading the story.

brim
The brim of something, like a jar, is the very top.

mellow
If someone is mellow, they are very relaxed and pleasant.

persnickety
If someone is persnickety, they are very picky about what they like.

compromise
When you make a compromise with someone, each of you agrees to do something or give up something to solve a problem together.

perseverance
Someone who has perseverance continues with something even though it is difficult.

Words About the Story

These words will be introduced after the story is read, using context from the story.

compile   motivate

Getting Ready for the Read-Aloud

Ask students to look at the picture of the boy on page 166. Read the title aloud. Tell students that the boy in the picture collects words.

Explain that people often collect things that have special meaning to them. Discuss with students the reasons why a person might collect words. Have them predict where the boy might find words for his collection and what he might do with these words.

The following words occur in the story. They can be briefly explained as you come to them in the story: *security guard*, a worker who keeps a building and the people in it safe; *lounge*, a place to sit and relax.

Donavan's Word Jar

By Monalisa DeGross

Illustrated by Susan Keeter

Like most of the kids in his class, Donavan liked to collect things. A few kids in his class collected rocks, insects, or stamps. Some other kids collected coins, comics, or baseball cards. Donavan's best friend, Eric, collected marbles. But when it came to collecting things, Donavan Allen was different. He had a collection like no one else he knew. Donavan collected words. Yes, words. He wrote his words in purple ink on yellow slips of paper. At the end of each day, he put the slips in a large, round glass jar.

Bringing the Story to Life

Ask students to write words they think are funny or interesting on slips of paper and put them in a classroom word jar. Invite students to add words from the story after reading and allow them to keep adding to their collection throughout the year.

mellow

How was Donavan like his classmates? How was he different from them?

All kinds of words went into Donavan's collection. He had big words like PROFOUND that made him feel smart. Little words like CUDDLE warmed his heart. Donavan found that soft words like HUSH soothed his fears. Silly words like SQUABBLE slipped off his tongue and tickled his ears. From somewhere he collected HIEROGLYPHIC, a strange word that made him wonder. And just for fun, he added strong words like WARRIOR, words that rang in his ears like thunder. Donavan put mysterious-sounding words like EXTRATERRESTRIAL into his collection. And there were musical-sounding words like ORCHESTRAL.

Collecting words was fun—they were everywhere.

Donavan collected so many words that his jar was jam-packed, filled to the **brim**, almost spilling over the rim, with words, words, and more words.

One Friday morning Donavan was putting a word into his jar when he realized that there was no more room. Donavan realized that this wasn't going to be an easy problem to solve. Then he remembered the one person who always had the greatest ideas of all. Later, Donavan was reading when he heard his father's footsteps in the hall. He picked up his jar and followed his father down the stairs and into the kitchen.

"How are you doing, partner?" his father asked.

"Fine." Donavan said quickly. Before his father could ask another question, Donavan rushed on. "Can I go over to Grandma's and visit? It's really important."

> Why did Donavan want to visit Grandma?

mellow

"Okay, but you watch yourself crossing the streets in the rain," his dad said. "And Donavan, why don't you ask your Grandma if she's free to come to dinner tonight? Tell her I'm doing the cooking," he added.

"I will," Donavan called over his shoulder.

Donavan pushed open the heavy glass doors to the **Mellow** View Apartments. He smiled at Mr. Bill Gut, the security guard, as he signed his name in the guest book. Donavan pushed the button and got onto the elevator. His grandma lived on the fourth floor. Donavan didn't like where Grandma lived now. Everyone there seemed so gloomy.

Donavan knocked on the apartment door and waited. When his grandma opened the door and saw him, she smiled.

"Donnie! What a pleasant surprise," Grandma said, opening the door wider. "It's nice to see you. Come in."

Donavan set his jar on the dining room table and explained his problem to his grandma. When he finished talking, he sat back in his chair and waited for her solution.

Grandma reached over and plucked a few slips of paper from Donavan's jar.

"Donnie," she said, "you sure have got yourself a treasure here. This is a wonderful collection of words." Donavan smiled and sat up a little straighter.

Grandma's praise made him feel good, but Donavan still needed a solution to his problem.

"Do you see my problem, Grandma?" he asked. "I thought of getting a larger jar, but that would only get full, too."

Grandma settled back in her chair. She didn't say anything for a long while, and Donavan began to feel a little uneasy. Maybe, just maybe, his grandma didn't have a solution. She dipped her hand back into the word jar and pulled out a few more words.

"There are some words in this jar that I know folks living here could use," she said. Donavan slipped to the edge of his chair and wondered what his grandma was going to say. She continued.

"Now, I like the word **PERSNICKETY**. That word fits Miz Marylou to a T. That woman has to have everything she does just right." Grandma slipped another word from the jar. "CANTANKEROUS— that's a perfect word for our guard, Bill Gut. I'll bet he argues with flies."

"I enjoyed your words, Donnie. I'm sure a lot of people would." She smiled at him and waited to see if he had something to say.

mellow

> How does Grandma suggest that Donavan use his words?

"Grandma, I'd be glad to let any of your friends see my words. But they couldn't keep them—I'd have to have them back for my collection." Donavan's voice was firm.

"Well, I am sorry if I didn't help you."

"Oh, Grandma, that's okay," Donavan answered, trying hard not to show his disappointment. He did not want to hurt his grandma's feelings.

Donavan picked up his word jar and tucked it firmly under his arm. Grandma walked with him to the door.

"Take care of yourself, 'Wordgatherer,'" she said, hugging him close.

In the elevator, Donavan thought about his word jar. It had taken months, weeks, days, and hours to fill it. Deciding which words to keep was hard. Then Donavan checked the spelling and made sure he understood what each new word meant. What had his grandma been thinking of? It seemed like she wanted him to just give his words away. He loved his word collection. But he had to think of a way to handle it, now that it was growing so large.

What did Donavan think of Grandma's suggestion?

mellow

The elevator doors opened, and Donavan stepped into the lounge. No one in the room was talking to or looking at each other, except Miz Marylou and Mr. Bill Gut.

They were standing at the security guard's desk arguing very loudly. No one else was paying any attention to them. As Donavan walked closer he could hear every word they said.

"Miz Marylou, this lounge will open or close when I say so," Mr. Bill Gut said in a gruff voice.

"Well, I am telling you, Bill, that's a mistake. That should be decided by the people who live here," she answered back.

"I'm the guard, and I say what goes on in this lounge," Mr. Bill Gut bellowed.

Donavan looked from one to the other. They both began to shout at the same time, since neither one was listening to what the other was saying. Donavan set his word jar on the corner of the desk and dug around inside the jar until he found a certain word. He tugged Miz Marylou's sleeve and then Mr. Bill's jacket. They both looked down, surprised to see Donavan standing there.

mellow

What was happening in the lounge when Donavan arrived there?

"I think you two need this word," Donavan said in a stern voice.

They both looked at the yellow slip of paper in Donavan's hand. Miz Marylou giggled, and Mr. Bill Gut smiled.

"Well, Marylou, what time do you think is a good time to open?" Mr. Bill Gut asked, scratching his head.

"Bill, I checked with a couple of people and they suggested ten o'clock. What do you think of that?" Miz Marylou asked, smiling at Mr. Bill Gut.

Donavan let out a loud sigh of relief. He had come at just the right time—they needed the word **COMPROMISE**.

Miz Marylou and Mr. Bill weren't shouting anymore. They were talking to each other quietly; they were coming to an agreement. That sure made Donavan feel good. His word had been just what they needed.

mellow

How did Donavan's word jar help Miz Marylou and Mr. Bill?

Donavan suddenly remembered that his father had asked him to invite Grandma to dinner. He ran back to the elevator and pushed the UP button.

"Back so soon?" Grandma asked, opening the door.

"I forgot to invite you to dinner tonight. Dad is going to cook. Do you want to come around?" Donavan asked.

"Well, I certainly do—in fact, why don't I just get my coat and walk with you?" Grandma suggested.

As they walked down the hall, Donavan began to tell Grandma about how he had helped Miz Marylou and Mr. Bill Gut.

When Grandma and Donavan got to the lounge, Donavan could not believe what he saw. Grandma's neighbors were up and around, laughing and talking. They all seemed excited. He looked around to see what was going on.

Donavan saw that they were waving little yellow slips of paper in their hands.

"MY WORDS! THEY HAVE MY WORDS!" Donavan shouted.

Mr. Avery was no longer slumped in front of the TV. He was tacking one of Donavan's words up on the bulletin board. Donavan looked over at the desk and saw Mrs. Agnes digging into his word jar. There were people in a line behind her laughing and talking. They were waiting to get a word from his jar.

"GRANDMA! STOP THEM. THEY ARE TAKING MY WORDS!" He turned to his grandma, but she looked just as surprised as he felt.

What was happening in the lounge when Donavan returned? How did Donavan feel about it?

mellow

"Donnie, calm down. They didn't know. You left the jar on the desk," she said in a quiet voice. Donavan couldn't stop what was happening.

Mr. Crawford, the mailman, passed Donavan and waved his word over his head. "**PERSEVERANCE**," he called out. "That's just the word I need. Some days I get so tired, I can hardly make it. I'm going to try just a little harder to keep going," he said, tucking the word in his shirt pocket.

"Wow! One of my words made Mr. Crawford feel better," Donavan said.

All around him, Grandma's neighbors were laughing and talking to each other. They had never acted so lively before.

Everyone wanted to thank him for sharing his words. Donavan felt as if the sun had come out inside him. Mr. Bill Gut pointed to the empty jar on the desk and said, "Looks like we cleaned you out, young fellow."

"Donnie, are all of your words gone?" asked Grandma. "Honey, I am so sorry, I know you didn't want to give your words away. Maybe you could ask for them back?" she said.

Donavan looked up at her and smiled.

"Grandma, they love my words, the words made them talk to each other."

> How did Donavan's feelings change as he watched Grandma's neighbors?

Grandma wrote on a slip of paper. "This is for you, 'Wordgatherer,' " Grandma said, her voice full of pride.

Donavan took the slip of paper. On one side it said "A happy accident," and on the other side the word SERENDIPITY was written.

Talking About the Story

- Have students review the story by describing Donavan's problem in their own words and explaining how the problem was solved.

- Encourage students to tell about collections they have. Ask them to tell when and how they started the collections. Invite them to describe some of the best pieces in their collections and ask them what they will do when their collections get too big.

Vocabulary in Action

brim

In the story Donavan's jar was filled to the brim. The brim of something, like a jar, is the very top.

- Ask which would make a mess if it were filled to the brim, a bathtub or a jar of peanut butter.
- Have a volunteer fill a paper cup to the brim with water.

persnickety

Grandma said Miz Marylou was persnickety. If someone is persnickety, they are very picky about what they like.

- Ask which a persnickety person would say more often, *I like that* or *I don't like that.* Why do you say that?
- Have volunteers show the actions of a persnickety eater.

mellow

The name of the place where Grandma lived was Mellow View. If someone is mellow, they are very relaxed and pleasant.

- Ask which might make you feel mellow, listening to quiet music or being caught in a thunderstorm. Why is that?
- Have students demonstrate how a mellow person would act if he had to wait in line at the supermarket.

perseverance

Mr. Crawford said he needed perseverance. Someone who has perseverance continues with something even though it is difficult.

- Ask which shows perseverance, a dog that keeps bringing its leash to its owner until it gets taken for a walk or a dog that lies in the sun and sleeps. Why?
- Ask students to show perseverance by continuing to build a tall tower with blocks, even when it has fallen several times.

compromise

Miz Marylou and Mr. Bill Gut compromise. When you make a compromise with someone, each of you agrees to do something or give up something to solve a problem together.

- Ask which is an example of compromise, demanding that your friend play your favorite game or agreeing to take turns playing your game and the one she likes. Explain why.
- Put a collection of items between two students. Ask them to work out a compromise for dividing the items.

motivate

Donavan's words motivated Miz Marylou and Mr. Bill Gut to find a way to get along better. To motivate means to make someone feel like they can do something difficult.

- Ask which is a way to motivate a child to clean up her room, saying *I know you can do a good job* or saying *What a mess!* Why do you think so?
- Invite each student to motivate a partner to do a thing that seems hard.

compile

Donavan compiled a collection of words. When you compile something, you bring together lots of things, such as pieces of information.

- Ask which would you compile, a mound of leaves or a list of friends' phone numbers. Explain why.
- Ask students to compile a list of their favorite foods.

Bibliography

Ada, Alma Flor. (1997). *The Lizard and the Sun.* Illustrated by Felipe Dávalos. New York: Random House.

Agard, John. (1988). *Brer Rabbit: The Great Tug-o-War.* Illustrated by Korky Paul. Hauppauge, NY: Barron's Educational Series.

Baer, Edith. (1980). *Words Are Like Faces.* New York: Random House.

Jane Goodall. (2003). Adapted from *Jane Goodall: A Good and True Heart,* by Ann Martin Bowler. Austin, TX: Steck-Vaughn.

Brooks, Erik. (2000). *The Practically Perfect Pajamas.* New York: Winslow House.

Cameron, Ann. (2002). "The Astronaut and the Onion," from *Gloria Rising.* Illustrated by Lis Toft. New York: Farrar, Straus & Giroux.

Cameron, Ann. (1981). "Gloria Who Might Be My Best Friend," from *The Stories Julian Tells.* New York: Knopf.

DeGross, Monalisa. (1994). *Donavan's Word Jar.* New York: Harper Collins.

Fetty, Margaret. (2003). *Sheila's New Sweater.* Austin, TX: Steck-Vaughn.

Forest, Heather. (1998). *Stone Soup.* Illustrated by Susan Gaber. Little Rock, AR: August House.

Hall, Martin. (1996) *Charlie and Tess.* Illustrated by Catherine Walters. Wauwatosa, WI: Little Tiger Press.

Harrison, Troon. (1999). *The Dream Collector.* Illustrated by Alan and Lea Daniel. Toronto: Kids Can Press.

Hoff, Lewis. (2003). *Harriet Hare Tells All.* Austin, TX: Steck-Vaughn.

Kline, Suzy. (2001). "Horrible Harry and the Brownie Revenge," from *School's In!* New York: Scholastic.

Medearis, Angela Shelf. (1994). *Annie's Gifts.* Illustrated by Anna Rich. Orange, N.J: Just Us Books.

Robson, Chelle. (2003). *Planting Opportunity.* Austin, TX: Steck-Vaughn.

Roth, David. (1988). "Nine Gold Medals." David Roth/Maythelight Music.

Rupp, Rochelle. (2003). *Returning the Enemy's Dog.* Austin, TX: Steck-Vaughn.

Soto, Gary. (1988). *Big Bushy Mustache.* Illustrated by Joe Cepeda. New York: Random House.

Starbird, Kaye. (1963). "Eat-It-All Elaine," from *Don't Ever Cross a Crocodile.* New York: HarperCollins.

Stevenson, James. (1998). *Sam the Zamboni Man.* Illustrated by Harvey Stevenson. New York: Greenwillow.

Tompert, Ann. (1997). *How Rabbit Lost His Tail.* Illustrated by Jacqueline Chwast. Boston: Houghton Mifflin Company.

Van Allsburg, Chris. (1983). *The Wreck of the Zephyr.* Boston: Houghton Mifflin Company.

Yolen, Jane. (1987). *Owl Moon.* Illustrated by John Schoenherr. New York: Penguin.

Additional Favorite Read-Alouds

Barber, Barbara, E. (1996). *Allie's Basketball Dream*. Illustrated by Darryl Ligasan. New York: Lee & Low Books.

Cowley, Joy. (1998). *Big Moon Tortilla*. Illustrated by Dyanne Strongbow. Honesdale, PA: Caroline House, Boyds Mill Press.

Duncan, Alice Faye. (1999). *Miss Viola and Uncle Ed Lee*. Illustrated by Catherine Stock. New York: Atheneum Books.

Foreman, Michael. (1996). *Seal Surfer*. San Diego: Harcourt.

Hamilton, Martha, & Weiss, Mitch. (1999). *How & Why Stories: World Tales Kids Can Read and Tell*. Little Rock, AR: August House.

Hoberman, Mary Ann. (1999). *And to Think That We Thought That We'd Never Be Friends*. Illustrated by Keven Hawkes. New York: Random House.

Hoberman, Mary Ann. (1997). *The Seven Silly Eaters*. Illustrated by Marla Frazee. San Diego: Harcourt.

Kimmel, Eric A. (1994). *Anansi and the Talking Melon*. Illustrated by Janet Stevens. New York: Holiday House.

Trivizas, Eugene. (1993). *Three Little Wolves and the Big Bad Pig*. Illustrated by Helen Oxenbury. New York: Atheneum Books.

Viorst, Judith. (1997). *Alexander and the Terrible, Horrible, No Good, Very Bad Day*. Illustrated by Ray Cruz. New York: Atheneum Books.